Contemptible

Contemptible

A Personal Recollection of the
'Retreat From Mons'
by a British Infantry Officer

Casualty

LEONAUR

Contemptible
A Personal Recollection of the 'Retreat From Mons' by a British Infantry Officer
by Casualty

First published under the title
"Contemptible"

Leonaur is an imprint of Oakpast Ltd

Copyright in this form © 2012 Oakpast Ltd

ISBN: 978-0-85706-872-9 (hardcover)
ISBN: 978-0-85706-873-6 (softcover)

http://www.leonaur.com

Publisher's Notes

Contents

Leaving England   7

Calm Before the Storm   12

The Advance to Mons   15

Mons   19

The Beginning of the Retreat   23

Darkness   27

Venérolles   30

St. Quentin and La Fère   33

Sir John French   37

A Pause, and More Marching   40

A Rear-Guard Action   44

Villiers-Cotterets   47

Heat and Dust   52

The Occupation of Villiers   55

The Last Lap   60

The Turn of the Tide   65

The Advance Begins   67

The Crossing of the Marne   71

An Advanced-Guard Action   74

Defence	79
The Defence of the Brandy	82
Strategy As You Like It	85
The Last Advance	90
Saturday Night	95
The Crossing of the Aisne	101
The Cellars of Poussey	107
The First Trenches	111
In Reserve at Souvir	116
To Straighten the Line	122
The Jaws of Death	126
The Field Hospital	132
Operation	137
St. Nazaire	141
Somewhere in Mayfair	143

CHAPTER 1

Leaving England

No cheers, no handkerchiefs, no bands. Nothing that even suggested the time-honoured scene of soldiers leaving home to fight the Empire's battles. Parade was at midnight. Except for the lighted windows of the barracks, and the rush of hurrying feet, all was dark and quiet. It was more like ordinary night operations than the dramatic departure of a unit of the First British Expeditionary Force to France.

As the battalion swung into the road, the subaltern could not help thinking that this was indeed a queer send-off. A few sergeants' wives, standing at the corner of the parade ground, were saying goodbye to their friends as they passed. "Goodbye, Bill;" "Good luck, Sam!" Not a hint of emotion in their voices. One might have thought that husbands and fathers went away to risk their lives in war every day of the week. And if the men were at all moved at leaving what had served for their home, they hid it remarkably well. Songs were soon breaking out from all parts of the column of route. As the club house, and then the Golf Club, stole silently up and disappeared behind him, the subaltern wondered whether he would ever see them again. But he refused to let his thoughts drift in this channel. Meanwhile, the weight of the mobilisation kit was almost intolerable.

In an hour the station was reached. An engine was shunting up and down, piecing the troop trains together, and in twenty minutes the battalion was shuffling down the platform, the empty trains on either side. Two companies were to go to each train, twelve men to a third-class compartment, N.C.O.s second class, officers first. As soon as the men were in their seats, the subaltern made his way to the seat he had "bagged," and prepared to go to sleep. Another fellow pushed his head through the window and wondered what had become of the regimental transport. Somebody else said he didn't know or care; his valise was always lost, he said; they always made a point of it.

Soon after, they were all asleep, and the train pulled slowly out of the station.

When the subaltern awoke it was early morning, and they were moving through Hampshire fields at a rather sober pace. He was assailed with a poignant feeling of annoyance and resentment that this war should be forced upon them. England looked so good in the morning sunshine, and the comforts of English civilisation were so hard to leave. The sinister uncertainty of the future brooded over them like a thunder cloud.

Isolated houses thickened into clusters, streets sprang up, and soon they were in Southampton.

The train pulled up at the Embarkation Station, quite close to the wharf to which some half-dozen steamers were moored. There was little or no delay. The battalion fell straight into "massed formation," and began immediately to move on to one of the ships. The colonel stood by the gangway talking to an embarkation officer. Everything was in perfect readiness, and the subaltern was soon able to secure a berth.

There was plenty of excitement on deck while the horses of the regimental transport were being shipped into the hold.

To induce "Light Draft," "Heavy Draft" horses and "Officers' Chargers"—in all some sixty animals—to trust themselves to be lowered into a dark and evil-smelling cavern, was no easy matter. Some shied from the gangway, neighing; other walked peaceably on to it, and, with a "thus far and no farther" expression in every line of their bodies, took up a firm stand, and had to be pushed into the hold with the combined weight of many men. Several of the transport section narrowly escaped death and mutilation at the hands, or rather hoofs, of the officers' chargers. Meanwhile a sentry, with fixed bayonet, was observed watching some lascars, who were engaged in getting the transport on board. It appeared that the wretched fellows, thinking that they were to be taken to France and forced to fight the Germans, had deserted to a man on the previous night, and had had to be routed out of their hiding-places in Southampton.

Not that such a small thing as that could upset for one moment the steady progress of the embarkation of the army. It was like a huge, slow-moving machine; there was a hint of the inexorable in its exactitude. Nothing had been forgotten—not even eggs for the officers' breakfast in the captain's cabin.

Meanwhile the other ships were filling up. By midday they began to slide down the Solent, and guesses were being freely exchanged about the destination of the little flotilla. Some said Boulogne, others Calais; but the general opinion was Havre, though nobody knew for certain, for the captain of the ship had not yet opened his sealed orders. The transports crept slowly along the coast of the Isle of Wight, but it was not until evening that the business of crossing the Channel was begun in earnest.

The day had been lovely, and officers and men had spent it mostly in sleeping and smoking upon the deck. Spirits had risen as the day grew older. For at dawn the cheeriest optimist is a pessimist, while at midday pessimists become optimists. In the early morning the German Army had been invincible. At lunch the battalion was going to Berlin, on the biggest holiday of its long life!

The subaltern, still suffering from the after-effects of inoculation against enteric, which had been unfortunately augmented by a premature indulgence in fruit, and by the inability to rest during the rush of mobilisation, did not spend a very happy night. The men fared even worse, for the smell of hot, cramped horses, steaming up from the lower deck, was almost unbearable. But their troubles were soon over, for by seven o'clock the boat was gliding through the crowded docks of Havre.

Naturally most of the mess had been in France before, but to Tommy it was a world undiscovered. The first impression made on the men was created by a huge negro working on the docks. He was greeted with roars of laughter, and cries of, "Hallo, Jack Johnson!" The red trousers of the French sentries, too, created a tremendous sensation. At length the right landing-stage was reached. Equipments were thrown on, and the battalion was paraded on the dock.

The march through the cobbled streets of Havre rapidly developed into a fiasco. This was one of the first, if not the very first, landing of British troops in France, and to the French it was a novelty, calling for a tremendous display of open-armed welcome. Children rushed from the houses, and fell upon the men crying for "souvenirs." Ladies pursued them with basins full of wine and what they were pleased to call beer. Men were literally carried from the ranks, under the eyes of their officers, and borne in triumph into houses and inns. What with the heat of the day and the heaviness of the equipment and the after-effects of the noisome deck, the men could scarcely be blamed for availing themselves of such hospitality, though to drink intoxicants on the march is suicidal. Men "fell out," first by ones and twos, then by whole half-dozens and dozens. The subaltern himself was scarcely strong enough to stagger up the long hills at the back of the town, let alone worrying about his men. The colonel was aghast, and very furious. He couldn't understand it. (He was riding.)

The camp was prepared for the troops in a wonderfully complete fashion—not the least thing seemed to have been forgotten. The men, stripped of their boots, coats and equipments, were resting in the shade of the tents. A caterer from Havre had come up to supply the mess, and the subaltern was able to procure from him a bottle of rather heady claret, which, as he was thirsty and exhausted, he consumed too rapidly, and found himself hopelessly inebriate. Luckily there was nothing to do, so he slept for many hours.

Waking up in the cool of the evening he heard the voices of another second-lieutenant and a reservist subaltern talking about some people he knew near his home. It was good to forget about wars and soldiers, and everything that filled so amply the present and future, and to lose himself in pleasant talk of pleasant things at home. . . . The dinner provided by the French caterer was very French, and altogether the last sort of meal that a young gentleman suffering from anti-enteric inoculation ought to have indulged in. Everything conspired to make him worse, and what with the heat and the malady, he spent a very miserable time.

After about two days' stay, the battalion moved away from the rest camp, and, setting out before dawn, marched back through those fatal streets of Havre, this time deserted in the moonlight, to a sort of shed, called by the French authorities a troop station. Here as usual the train was waiting, and the men had but to be put in. The carriages could not be called luxurious; to be frank, they were cattle-trucks. But it takes more than that to damp the spirits of Mr. Thomas Atkins. Cries imitating the lowing of cattle and the bleating of sheep broke out from the trucks!

The train moved out of the depôt, and wended its way in the most casual manner through the streets of Havre. This so amused Tommy that he roared with laughter. The people who rushed to give the train a send-off, with many cries of "*Vive les Anglais,*" "*A bas les Bosches,*" were greeted with more bleatings and brayings.

★★★★★★

The journey through France was quite uneventful. Sleeping or reading the whole day through, the subaltern only remembered

Rouen, passed at about midday, and Amiens later in the evening. The train had paused at numerous villages on its way, and in every case there had been violent demonstrations of enthusiasm. In one case a young lady of prepossessing appearance had thrust her face through the window, and talked very excitedly and quite incomprehensibly, until one of the fellows in the carriage grasped the situation, leant forward, and did honour to the occasion. The damsel retired blushing.

At Amiens various rumours were afloat. Somebody had heard the colonel say the magic word "Liège." Pictures of battles to be fought that very night thrilled some of them not a little.

★★★★★★

Dawn found the battalion hungry, shivering and miserable, paraded by the side of the track, at a little wayside station called Wassigné. The train shunted away, leaving the battalion with a positive feeling of desolation. A staff officer, rubbing sleep from his eyes, emerged from a little "*estaminet*" and gave the colonel the necessary orders. During the march that ensued the battalion passed through villages where the three other regiments in the brigade were billeted. At length a village called Iron was reached, and their various billets were allotted to each company.

The subaltern's company settled down in a huge water-mill; its officers being quartered in the miller's private house.

A wash, a shave and a meal worked wonders.

And so the journey was finished, and the battalion found itself at length in the theatre of operations.

★★★★★★

I have tried in this chapter to give some idea of the ease and smoothness with which this delicate operation of transportation was carried out. The battalions which composed the First Expeditionary Force had been spread in small groups over the whole length and breadth of Britain. They had been mobilised, embarked, piloted across the Channel in the face of an undefeated enemy fleet, rested, and trained to their various areas of concentration, to take their place by the side of their French Allies.

All this was accomplished without a single hitch, and with a speed that was astonishing. When the time comes for the inner history of the war to be written, no doubt proper praise for these preliminary arrangements will be given to those who so eminently deserve it.

CHAPTER 2

Calm Before the Storm

Peace reigned for the next five days, the last taste of careless days that so many of those poor fellows were to have.

A route march generally occupied the mornings, and a musketry parade the evenings. Meanwhile, the men were rapidly accustoming themselves to the new conditions. The officers occupied themselves with polishing up their French, and getting a hold upon the reservists who had joined the battalion on mobilisation.

The French did everything in their power to make the battalion at home. Cider was given to the men in buckets. The officers were treated like the best friends of the families with whom they were billeted. The fatted calf was not spared, and this in a land where there were not too many fatted calves.

The company "struck a particularly soft spot." The miller had gone to the war leaving behind him his wife, his mother and two children. Nothing they could do for the five officers of the company was too much trouble. *Madame Mère* resigned her bedroom to the major and his second in command, while *madame* herself slew the fattest of her chickens and rabbits for the meals of her hungry officers.

The talk that was indulged in must have been interesting, even though the French was halting and ungrammatical. Of all the companies' messes, this one took the most serious view of the future, and earned for itself the nickname of "*Les Misérables.*" The senior subaltern said openly that this calm preceded a storm. The papers they got—*Le Petit Parisian* and such like—talked vaguely of a successful offensive on the extreme right: Mülhouse, it was said, had been taken. But of the left, of Belgium, there was silence. Such ideas as the subaltern himself had on the strategical situation were but crude. The line of battle, he fancied, would stretch north and south, from Mülhouse to Liège. If it were true that Liège had fallen, he thought the left would rest successfully on Namur. The English Army, he imagined, was acting as "general reserve," behind the French line, and would not be employed until the time had arrived to hurl the last reserve into the *mêlée*, at the most critical point.

And all the while, never a sound of firing, never a sight of the red and blue of the French uniforms. The war might have been two hundred miles away!

Meanwhile Tommy on his marches was discovering things. Wonder of wonders, this curious people called "baccy" *tabac!* "And if yer wants a bit of bread yer awsks for pain, strewth!" He loved to hear the French gabble to him in their excited way; he never thought that reciprocally his talk was just as funny. The French matches earned unprintable names. But on the whole he admired sunny France with its squares of golden corn and vegetables, and when he passed a painted crucifix with its cluster of flowering graves, he would say: "Golly, Bill, ain't it pretty? We oughter 'ave them at 'ome, yer know." And of course he kept on saying what he was going to do with "*Kayser* Bill."

One night after the evening meal, the men of the company gave a little concert outside the mill. The flower-scented twilight was fragrantly beautiful, and the mill stream gurgled a lullaby accompaniment as it swept past the trailing grass. Nor was there any lack of talent. One reservist, a miner since he had left the army, roared out several songs concerning the feminine element at the seaside, or voicing an inquiry as to a gentleman's companion on the previous night. Then, with an entire lack of appropriateness, another got up and recited "*The Wreck of the Titanic*" in a most touching and dramatic manner. Followed a song with a much appreciated chorus—

> *Though your heart may ache awhile,*
> *Never mind!*
> *Though your face may lose its smile,*
> *Never mind!*
> *For there's sunshine after rain,*
> *And then gladness follows pain,*
> *You'll be happy once again,*
> *Never mind!*

The ditty deals with broken vows, and faithless hearts, and blighted lives; just the sort of song that Tommy loves to warble after a good meal in the evening. It conjured to the subaltern's eyes the picture of the dainty little star who had sung it on the boards of the Coliseum. And to conclude, *madame's* voice, French, and sonorously metallic, was heard in the dining-room striking up the "*Marseillaise*." Tommy did not know a word of it, but he yelled "March on" (a very good translation of "*Marchons*") and sang "*lar lar*" to the rest of the tune.

Thus passed peacefully enough those five days—the calm before the storm.

CHAPTER 3

The Advance to Mons

The battalion had arrived at Iron on a Sunday morning. It had rested there, while the remainder of the British Army was being concentrated, until Friday morning. On Thursday night the battalion orders made it clear that a start was to be made. Parade was to be earlier than usual, and nothing was to be left behind. Everyone was very sorry to be leaving their French friends, and there were great doings that night. Champagne was produced, and a horrible sort of liquor called "*alcahol*" was introduced into the coffee. Such was the generosity of the miller's people that it was only with the greatest difficulty that the captain induced *madame* to accept any payment for her kindness. And so in the chill of that Friday morning the battalion marched away, not without many handshakings and blessings from the simple villagers. The subaltern often wonders what became of *mesdames*, and that excitable son Raoul, and charming Thérèse, whom the subalterns had all insisted on kissing before they left. A very different sort of folk occupy that village now. He only hopes that his friends escaped them.

The battalion joined its brigade, and the brigade its division, and before the sun was very high in the sky they were swinging along the "*route nationale*," due northwards. The day was very hot, and the battalion was hurried, with as short halts as possible, towards Landrécies. As, however, this march was easily surpassed in "frightfulness" by many others, it will be enough to say that Landrécies was reached in the afternoon.

Having seen his men as comfortable as possible in the schools where they were billeted for the night, the subaltern threw off his equipment, and having bought as much chocolate as he and a friend could lay their hands on, retired to his room and lay down.

At about seven o'clock in the evening the three subalterns made their way to the largest hotel in the town, where they found the rest of the mess already assembled at dinner. He often remembered this meal afterwards, for it was the last that he had properly served for some time. In the middle of it the colonel was summoned hastily away by an urgent message, and before they dispersed to their billets, the unwelcome news was received that battalion parade was to be at three o'clock next morning.

"This," said he, "is the real beginning of the show. Henceforth, horribleness."

A hunk of bread eaten during the first stage of the march was all the breakfast he could find. Maroilles, a suburb of Landrécies, was passed, and an hour later a big railway junction. The march seemed to be directed on Mauberge, but a digression was made to the northwest, and finally a halt was called at a tiny village called Harignes. The subaltern's men were billeted in a large barn opening on to an orchard.

After a scrap meal, he pulled out some maps to study the country which lay before them, and what should meet his eye but the field of Waterloo, with all its familiar names: Charleroi, Ligny, Quatrebras, Genappes, the names which he had studied a year ago at Sandhurst. Surely these names of the victory of ninety-nine years ago were a good omen!

"You've only left Sandhurst a year, you ought to know all about this country," someone told him.

A horrible rumour went about that another move was to be made at five o'clock the same evening, but this hour was subsequently altered to two o'clock the next morning. That night a five-*franc* postal order was given to every man as part of his pay.

Even in the height of summer there is always a feeling of ghostliness about nocturnal parades. The darkness was intense. As might be expected, the men had not by any means recovered from the heat and exertion of the previous day, and were not in the best of tempers. The subaltern himself was so tired that he had to lie down on the cold road at each hourly halt of ten minutes, and, with his cap for a pillow, sleep soundly for at least eight of those minutes. Then whistles were sounded ahead, the men would rise wearily, and shuffle on their equipment with the single effort that is the hall-mark of a well-trained soldier. The captain, passing along the company, called his attention to the village they were passing. It was Malplâquet. The grey light of dawn revealed large open fields. "I expect this is where they fought it out," said the captain.

Keeping a close eye upon the map, he could tell almost to a hundred yards where the boundary of Belgium crossed the road. A few miles further, a halt for breakfast was ordered, as it was about eight o'clock. The colonel called for company commanders, and while they were away Sir John French, followed by Sir Archibald Murray and a few members of the general staff, passed by in motors.

Amongst the hundred-and-one pictures that the subaltern will always carry in his mind of the opening stages of the campaign, this one stands out most vividly. The sun was shining, but it was still cool. On the right of the road was a thick forest of young firs; on the left, a row of essentially suburban villas were being built, curiously out of place in that agricultural district. The men were sitting on the banks of the road, or clustered round the "cookers," drawing their breakfast rations of bread and cold bacon. Then the major came back. There was an expression on his face that showed he was well aware of the dramatic part he was about to play.

Imagine him standing by the wayside, surrounded by his officers, two sergeant-majors, and some half-dozen senior sergeants, all with pencils ready poised to write his orders in their field service note-books. There was a pause of several seconds. The major seemed to be at a loss quite how to begin. "There's a lot that I needn't mention, but this is what concerns this company," he said with a jerk. "When we reach" (here he mentioned a name which the subaltern has long since forgotten) "we have to deploy to the left, and search the village of Harmigné to drive the enemy from it, and take up a position. . . ."

It was a blow. Officers were frowning over their note-books as if afraid they had not heard correctly. The enemy here, in the western corner of Belgium? The major's orders petered out. They saluted, and returned to their platoons, feeling puzzled and a little shaken.

The subaltern had come to this campaign with such fresh hopes of victory. This was not to have been a repetition of '70! France would not have gone to war unless she had been strong and ready. Inspired with the spirit of the First Republic, the French armies, they had told themselves, would surge forward in a wave of victory and beat successfully against the crumbling sands of the *Kaiser's* military monarchy—Victory, drenching Germany with the blood of her sons, and adding a lustre to the Sun of Peace that should never be dimmed by the black clouds of Militarism! And all this was not to be? He had never even heard that Liège had fallen, let alone Brussels, and here were the

Germans apparently right round the Allied flank. It was astounding, irritating. In a vague way he felt deceived and staggered. It was a disillusionment! If the Germans were across the Sambre, the French could scarcely launch their victorious attack on the Rhine.

The excitement dispelled his fatigue, but the men were openly incredulous. "The ruddy 'Oolans 'ere a'ready! They're only tellin' us that, to make us march!"

The first fight! How would it turn out? How would the men shape? Could the ammunition supply be depended upon? But above all, what would he be like? Would he feel afraid? If so, would he be able to hide it? Would his men follow him well? Perhaps he might be wounded (parts of him shrank from the thought), or killed. No, somehow he felt it was impossible that he would be killed. These and a thousand more such questions flashed through his brain as the march continued northwards.

The hourly halts were decreased from ten to about three minutes. The excitement of the future dissolved the accumulating fatigue of the three days. The very weight of his sword and haversack was forgotten.

It was Sunday morning. The bells of the village churches were ringing, and the women and children, decked in their Sunday best, were going calmly to church, just as if the greatest battle that, up to then, history had ever seen were not about to be fought around their very homesteads.

A waterworks was passed, and at last the crossroads were reached. There was a wait while the battalion in front of them deployed. Officers were loading their revolvers, the men charging their magazines. One company left as advanced guard, and very soon the battalion was on its way to its appointed sector of the battlefield.

They threw aside a hastily improvised barricade of ploughshares, and hurried on to the little village which was to be their especial care in the impending battle, known rather inadequately as "Mons."

CHAPTER 4

Mons

Then came the village of Harmigné—just a few cottages on either side of the road, and soon the companies debouched from the village to take up the positions allotted to them.

In war it is well known that he who sees most is likely to take least away. It was not the soldier's duty to gaze about him to see what was happening. He must enlarge his bit of trench, and be ready to meet the enemy when he himself is attacked. Therefore, if you ask a veteran of Mons about the battle, all he will be able to tell you as likely as not is, "Marching, and digging, and then marching mostly, sir."

The company on the left was astride a railway embankment in front of a large mine. The subaltern's company was directly in front of the village itself; another company to the right, the fourth in local reserve. The work of entrenchment began immediately. There was not time to construct a trench, as laid down in the manual of field engineering. Each man had to scrape with his entrenching tool as big a hole as he could before the enemy came upon him.

The subaltern had many things to arrange. The "field of fire" had to be "cleared," any refuge behind which the enemy might lurk within two hundred yards of the trenches had to be, if possible, cut down. Sheaves of corn standing upright presented the first problem for the defence. Should he burn as many of them as he could, or overturn them, or beat them down? No, sheaves were not bullet-proof. A man could be shot behind them just as easily as in the open. Moreover, they would serve to hide from the enemy artillery the exact lie of his lines. The position of his trenches, or rather holes, was about a hundred yards in front of the village, as it would be the first thing that the German artillery would "search." The range-taker took the ranges from the trenches to all prominent objects in front, with an instrument called the "Barr and Stroud." He then made these figures known to the four section commanders of the platoon, who in turn communicated them to their men.

Then he had to get in touch with the commanders on either side, and to send off a small party to improve what natural obstacles—in this case wire fences—lay in front. He next went to arrange for the methods of effecting a retirement, if it should be necessary, breaking through one or two fences so that this could be effected in perfect order. As some of the houses were still occupied, he went to the owners, and not knowing the French for pick and shovel, said: "*Monsieur, voulez vous me prêter des choses pour faire des troux dans la terre?*" illustrating it with pantomime. "*Ah, oui, Monsieur, des pioches!*" As many of these as possible were sent forward to the men, together with many pounds of biscuits which he brought from a shop, and buckets of water for the wounded.

So busy had he been that he had almost been unable to interest himself in the battle which was already beginning to develop on the left. While he was in the village a stretcher was carried through. The body on it was covered with a mackintosh sheet, but the man's face was visible, and if he had not been so busily occupied, the ashen face might have upset him a little. It was absolutely calm, and its expression was contorted neither by pain nor hate nor fear—the face of one who was indifferent, and very, very weak.

With that he returned to the trenches. "'Ere yer are, sir, I've started this 'un for yer," one man shouted. He threw off his equipment, and began to dig as he had never dug before. Each spadeful was safety for another inch of his body. It was fighting against time for protection of life and limb. The work was engrossing, exhilarating. Some of the men were too tired, too apathetic, too lazy to dig trenches as deep as they might have done. They had to be urged, cajoled, enticed, ordered.

The day was beautiful, hotter a great deal than those the men were accustomed to. The senior subaltern had been occupying a small hut as an advanced post. The enemy came within his range in some force, but having the presence of mind to restrain his men from firing, he managed to withdraw without loss. All the while the cavalry were being rapidly driven in.

This was about three o'clock, and the sound of a terrific bombardment could be heard from some miles to the left. This puzzled them, as it was naturally expected that the battle would develop from the north-east. The regiment on the right had been occupying a small copse; this was set alight to the rear of them, and they were forced to draw back through it, which must have been a terrible operation.

Fresh meat, in the form of a stew, was brought out to the trenches at about three o'clock. The bombardment on the left, like a terrific thunderstorm, rolled on till dusk. A few aeroplanes flew overhead, looking like huge birds in the blue sky. As yet the troops found it very hard to distinguish the Germans from the English, although several pamphlets had been issued on the subject.

As evening drew on, the trenches began to assume a more workmanlike aspect, although when one got down deeper than three feet the ground was like chalk and very difficult to cut.

Thus ended that memorable Sunday, when the English line, the last hope of the French, was pierced at Mons, when the appearance of a huge force, above all strong in cavalry, appeared on the left of the English line, and rendered the whole strategic position of the Allies so dangerous, that there was nothing for it but to fall back in order to avert a terrible catastrophe.

To ensure against surprise, he posted three sentry groups to his front. They had not been out more than half-an-hour before a huge fusillade broke out along the whole line. The groups had the greatest difficulty in crawling back to the trenches without being shot down in mistake for the enemy. He saw that this "peace method" would have to be given up; sentries in future would have to remain in the trenches.

Intermittently throughout the whole night firing continued. A searchlight had been played continually on the lines, and if anything, the artillery duel began before it was light.

This was his first opportunity to watch shell fire. The shells sailed overhead so slowly that he half expected to see them in their flight. The noise they made was very difficult to describe. They hurtled, they whizzed, they shrieked, they sang. He could imagine the thing spinning in its flight, creating a noise something like steam escaping jerkily from an engine.

An English battery was firing from somewhere unseen on the right, to meet an attack apparently launched on the left. Furious messages were passed up the line that the artillery were firing on their own men, and whether this was true or not, soon afterwards the attack ceased.

At about seven o'clock the major gave orders to withdraw his platoon when the company on his right should retire. This surprised him; for, knowing nothing of the general situation, he had felt that they would hang on, and fight the battle out then and there, to the last gasp. He gave orders to his section commanders, and then lay down to await the development of events.

At about nine o'clock a general retirement seemed to be taking place on the right. It is a very difficult thing to pick upon exactly the right moment to retire. If you retire too early, you allow the enemy to advance without having inflicted sufficient loss, *i.e.* you allow him to succeed too cheaply, to say nothing of rendering the position of units on your flanks precarious. On the other hand, if you hang on to your position too long, you become committed to a close fight, from which it is almost impossible to withdraw without the most serious losses.

There are no hedges in Belgium; the ground was perfectly open, and the subaltern could easily see what was happening on the right. It seemed to him that some unit delayed too long, for the rest of the line showed signs of envelopment. Eventually, however, the retirement to the village was effected quietly, and without loss. He led his platoon to a second defensive position about a mile behind the village, but already shells were beginning to drop around, and even beyond it.

CHAPTER 5

The Beginning of the Retreat

It was from this point that the great "Retreat from Mons" really began. The road in front of the battalion was hit by one or two shells. Apparently it was being "searched," and so the battalion was hastily moved into the open fields, assuming what is known as "Artillery Formation," *i.e.* small collections of troops, moving on the same objective, with "irregular distances and depths." By this means many lives must have been saved. After about a mile of very hurried marching, through turnip fields and stubble, the road was again reached, and the battalion was apparently out of the enemy's range.

The heat was beginning to be intense. The men had marched for the last three days almost incessantly, and without sufficient sleep. Sunday night in the firing-line had been full of excitement of battle, and all Monday morning had been spent at digging trenches. Imagine the state of the men! Dirty from digging, with a four days' growth of beard, bathed in sweat, eyes half closed with want of sleep, "packs" missing, lurching with the drunken torpor of fatigue, their own mothers would not have known them! There was no time to rest and sleep, when rest and sleep were the most desirable things on earth. Those men assuredly knew all the agonies of a temptation to sell for a few moments' sleep their liberty and lives.

During a halt the subaltern threw himself so heavily in a cabbage patch, that his revolver became unhitched from his belt, and when the halt was over he lurched to his feet and on, without noticing its loss. Careless? Perhaps, but one of his men lost his rifle and never noticed it, because he was carrying a spade!

There was, however, one consolation. The Germans had for the time been shaken off; although the noise of battle could still be heard uncomfortably near on the left. But if one waits long enough, the hottest sun must go to rest, and drag its horrible day with it. About six o'clock the battalion at last came up with its "cookers" and transport. Glory of glories, rest had at last been achieved! Never had bacon been so welcome, never tea so desirable, so stimulating, so wonderful.

The quartermaster-sergeant had some terrifying tales for the company mess about disasters on less fortunate parts of the line; but there was no time to go into the matter, for the battalion was ordered to parade immediately. This was the last straw! The men had been looking forward to, and longing for a good sleep that night. Every aching limb of their bodies cried out for rest, and here they were going to be put on outpost duty for yet another night. Imagine their state of mind! Is there a word to cope with the situation? Assuredly not, though great efforts were made! Darkness fell so swiftly that the officers had scarcely time to "site" the position of their trenches. Then the weary business of entrenching began again. Have you ever heard the tinkering, tapping, thudding sounds made by entrenching implements or spades? None of the men who heard it that night will ever forget it. It will give them a memory of energy, promoted by the desire for safety, clogged by heat and fatigue.

At about eleven or twelve at night a fair cover had been made, and the long-sought rest became possible at last—not, however, the sleep that the subaltern had been longing for all day, not complete oblivion to body and mind, for the fear of surprise was upon him even in his sleep, and he knew that if his precautions should prove insufficient, he would have to answer for sixty good lives. In addition there was the cold of the cloudless night, and the clinging wetness of the dew. These things would not have allowed him to sleep, even if he could.

A fresh day began very similar to the last. There were no signs of the enemy to the immediate front, so the work of entrenching continued. A "fatigue party" went to draw rations, which were distributed at about seven o'clock. This was their first introduction to "bully" beef and hard biscuits. Also, wonder of wonders, a "mail" was distributed.

He was lying in the corn just beginning to eat a biscuit and read a letter, when the voice of the senior subaltern called him from somewhere up the line. Thinking that he had got another letter, or something of that sort, he did not wait to put letters and rations in his haversack, but went straight to his senior. "A party of Uhlans, about 100 strong, have broken through the line further up. We have got to prevent them from taking us by surprise on this flank. So you had better take a couple of sections to keep them off." Commands on the battlefield must never be didactic and narrow. Tell a man what to do, give him his mission, and how he will carry it out, the methods he will employ, are for himself to determine.

He hurriedly collected his men and took up a position astride a road that ran behind, parallel to the lines. In peace-time manoeuvres one had generally been told the direction from which to expect the enemy, hours before he actually came; now, when the great game was being played in real earnest, he found that he had to guess. The Uhlans might have come unsuspecting along the road, in which case the game would be his; or they might come blundering along from somewhere in the rear and enfilade him, in which case the game would most assuredly be theirs. Fortunately, the Uhlans did not come at all.

Meanwhile a very rare and lucky circumstance was beginning to be apparent. The enemy were actually attacking from the direction they were expected! But this was only to be a rear-guard action, so he never saw his rations or letters again, after all.

The senior subaltern was left to "hold out" in a small cottage in the firing-line until the rest had "got away." With characteristic forethought and presence of mind he not only got his men away without loss, but seized all luxuries in the place!

As on the day before, in getting clear away from the enemy, the company had to pass a large stretch of ground which was being literally peppered with shrapnel. The noise was louder than it had seemed on the previous day. Thunder seemed muffled beside it. Moreover, thunder rolled—seemed to spread itself into space—but not so with bursting shells. The clap of sound caused by one is more confined, more localised, more intense. The earth seems to quiver under it. It suggests splitting, a terrible splitting. Only the nerves of the young and healthy can stand it. It would not be so bad if one could see the thing whistling through the air, or even when it bursts; but one cannot. After the crash a man may scream or moan, totter and fall, but for all one can see he might have been struck down by the wrath of God.

The road safely reached, the retreat was continued, but under very trying circumstances for the company. The brigadier in charge of the rear-guard action, not having sufficient cavalry at his disposal, ordered the company to take up the *rôle* of flank-guard to the retreating column. The company, extended over a long front, had to move across rough country, intersected with all sorts of obstacles, at the same rate as the infantry on the road, "*which*," as Euclid says, "*is impossible*." In war, however, the logically "impossible" is not impossible really, only very fatiguing.

Things grew from bad to worse. The men could no longer keep their places in the ranks. If one had seen them and not known the spirit of the British Army, one would have thought that they were a dispirited, defeated rabble. Yet, in their own minds, the officers and men had no doubts about what was going to happen: they were going to fight even though they might not sleep; and their determination was shaken not one whit.

There was a very welcome halt for an hour in the town, for the men to fill their water-bottles and rest.

The men's feet were beginning to suffer terribly, for the road along which they were marching had been cobbled—cobbles, not as we know them in England, but rounded on the surface—cobbles that turned one's ankles, cobbles that the nails of one's boots slipped on, that were metallic, that "gave" not the fraction of a millimetre. The hob-nails in the subaltern's boots began to press through the soles. To put his feet to the ground was an agony, and they swelled with the pain and heat. The bones of them ached with bearing his weight. They longed for air, to be dangling in some cool, babbling stream.

The mental strain of the morning's action was as nothing compared to the physical pain of the afternoon. The colonel, seeing his plight, offered to lend him his horse, but he thanked him and declined, as there is a sort of grim pride in "sticking it." The men, too, took an unreasonable objection to seeing their officers avail themselves of these lifts. Then the heavens were kind, and it rained; they turned faces to the clouds and let the drops fall on their features, unshaven, glazed with the sun, and clammy with sweat. They took off their hats and extended the palms of their hands. It was refreshing, invigorating, a tonic.

Somebody had heard the general say that they should have a rest, a real rest, that night. High hopes filled weary hearts. It got about that they were to be billeted in that suburb of Landrécies through which they had passed, Maroilles.

CHAPTER 6

Darkness

At about five o'clock on that aching day, Maroilles was reached. All through the streets there were halts and delays, intolerable to those in whom the want of rest had become a positive passion. At last the members of the billeting party were sighted—here at last was rest and sleep. . . .

Many a slip 'twixt cup and lip! The general, followed by the brigade-major and an orderly, came trotting down the road. A few hasty commands were thrown at the adjutant, accompanied by gesticulations towards the road leading out of the town. Assuredly some fresh devilment was rife, and for the moment, anyway, the cup had slipped. An attack on the town was expected by a large detachment of cavalry. The wretched men had to be hurried out, to line a row of hedges to the west of the town. They waited about half-an-hour, but saw not a sign of the famous square-crested Uhlan helmet. It appeared that the enemy had been content with destroying the canal bridge, which formed the communication between Maroilles and Landrécies, and had then withdrawn. There was a whole brigade in Maroilles, which was therefore cut off from the rest of the division, and from its natural line of retreat. That, however, did not greatly upset the rank and file, and billets were at last achieved.

The subaltern found that he was billeted in the same house as the headquarters of the battalion—colonel, second in command, adjutant, etc. His servant brought him his valise from the regimental transport, and he began to change the offending boots for a fresh pair, without nails.

Someone procured a footbath, and ablutions began.

The medical officer came in to say that the colonel seemed to be very ill. The subaltern was glad he had declined the offer of his horse.

He then began to shave and wash. Just as he was in the middle of this, with his boots and puttees off, his captain came in to say that his platoon was being sent off as infantry escort to a battery of artillery. By the time he had redressed himself, the battery and his platoon had both gone. The streets were filled by French peasants, as usual excited and garrulous, and by men settling down to their billets. The subaltern failed absolutely to discover what route his platoon had taken, but pursuing the road along which they had come, he soon left the town.

It was raining and blowing most fiercely; the darkness was intense, otherwise absolute silence reigned. Suddenly, excitedly, a voice, saturated with fear, cried out from the darkness, "Who goes there?" A face, with a bayonet in front of it, loomed up from the side of the road.

"Friend!" this tersely. "Sentry, have you seen a battery of artillery and a platoon of ——shires pass here?"

"No, sir; you're nearly in the outpost line. There's only Royal Blankshires in front, sir."

So they had evidently not come this way. Where next? They must be found. He felt that to lose his men would be a sort of dishonour. Even while he was thinking, a shout was wafted on the wind out of the darkness and chasing it, overtaking it almost, a rifle shot. It was as if a match had been applied to the whole line. With the rapidity of wind the crackling spread to either side.

Soon the whole line in front was blazing away into the darkness. Should the subaltern stop and try to lend assistance where he was, or hurry back to his own unit? Before long a couple of men rushed along the road crying out for stretcher bearers, and he learnt from one of them that in the darkness and confusion of the retreat, British had been fighting with British. The pitch darkness shrouded every action with a ghastly uncertainty.

Then news came through that another bridge had been captured. A fresh company arrived in reinforcement. There was nothing for it but to effect a retreat before the morning light could betray their weakness to the Germans. Apparently, however, the capture of the bridge had only been a precautionary measure, for the enemy did not press his attack home.

The subaltern saw that the best thing he could do would be to return to the remainder of his battalion at Maroilles. If he were to grope about the countryside in the dark, looking for "that battery," he would most likely be shot down for a spy; moreover, in a little over two hours the morning would dawn. So he trudged back to Maroilles.

He felt that he ought to have been on the verge of exhaustion from lack of food and from fatigue, and he vaguely wondered why he was not. The truth was that the excitement of the attack, coupled with the chill of the night, had restored him in mind and body, although he had marched over twenty miles on the previous day, had had no sleep that night, and no meal since the evening of the Battle of Mons.

The battalion was taking its rest as well as it could on the pavement of the street, so as to be ready to move at a minute's notice. The subaltern found his major, and reported that he had failed to find his platoon. The major was too sleepy to be annoyed. "I expect they'll turn up," he said. "We got some food in that house there; I should go and see if there is any left, if I were you."

Followed a couple of hours or so of interrupted sleep, disturbed by the cold. Then came dawn, and with it the shells whizzing and bursting over the town.

The retreat of the brigade had been cut off by the breaking of the canal bridge the previous evening, so the battalion had to retire to the east, and not to the west. As the subaltern marched along he reflected with grim amusement on the ease with which the most confirmed Sybarite can get accustomed to hardships. At home, if he did anything early on an empty stomach, he very soon felt faint and tired. Now, this was taken as a matter of course; one was only too glad to restore the circulation to the limbs, cramped with the cold and damp of dawn.

An hour or so later they ran into a French battalion, apparently preparing to occupy an outpost position along the bank of the road. This was a cheering sight. Tommy, who had expected to fight mixed up in some weird way with "*le petit Piou-Piou*," had not yet seen a Frenchman in action. In a vague way he fancied that "the Frenchies" had "let him down." He knew nothing of the battles of Charleroi and Namur, nor of the defence of Verdun, and the French were getting dreadfully unpopular with him. Things were thrown at any one who ventured to sing the "*Marseillaise*."

"Oh, '*ere* they are; so they '*ave* come. Well, that's somethink."

The "Marseillaise" broke out once again.

"Look 'ere, Bill, there's too much of this ruddy '*Marslasie*' abaht this 'ere show."

"'Ow d'you mean, Sam?"

"Why, it's all 'March on, March on.' I'm ruddy sick of it!"

CHAPTER 7

Venérolles

At this point the battalion turned in a south-westerly direction, passing through a village in which the French and English Head-quarters were quartered in "*estaminets*" on either side of the road. No doubt both were prosecuting their work equally successfully, but the subaltern could not help remarking the quietness of the one, and the excitement, volubility, and apparent confusion of the other. Still, he thought, different people have different ways of doing things.

Apparently to compensate for having no breakfast, the battalion was halted in an orchard. The men filled their haversacks with apples and pears, and consumed scarcely ripe plums with an avidity that made the officers fear that at least half of the battalion would be in the grip of colic before the night.

Because it was a cloudy day, or perhaps because one reaches a second heat in physical and mental fatigue, the subaltern did not feel so bad that day. The men, too, recovered their spirits. He began to think it was good to march on an empty stomach. The sight of French cavalry with their holland-covered helmets and curved sabres, suggested ample support. This would mean at least a rest before the next fight, he told himself.

These "*drâgons*" seemed exceedingly intelligent and superior men. They were quite preoccupied, like men who are going to do something. There was none of that inane shouting "*A bas les Bosches*." Later on, some transport columns were passed, and the men descended from their wagons and distributed bread to the English.

All day long the sound of guns rolled along to the right. The sound seemed to move parallel to them, otherwise the day's march was uneventful. At about half-past five in the evening the battalion suddenly struck the "*route nationale*," along which they had advanced north of

Etreux. There had been a feeling, once again, that the enemy had been successfully shaken off by the rapidity of the retreat.

Once again came disillusionment, for here were the guards' brigade entrenching themselves for the night. Apparently there had been very severe fighting around Etreux, which had resulted in a check to the enemy, for the moment, at any rate. The regiment, however, passed through Etreux, and was eventually ordered to occupy a defensive position around the village of Venérolles. Darkness fell so suddenly that the company commanders had the greatest difficulty in selecting good positions. Eventually the subaltern's platoon was placed astride a sunken lane, along the edge of an orchard. The position was a happy one, and since the hedge that stretched along its front was thick and about ten feet high, it seemed safe from surprise.

It was now quite dark, and the men had not had a meal since the few biscuits which had been given out in the early morning. At last, however, the regimental transport was heard creaking up the small lane which led to the position. Then the trouble began. The road was dark, deeply rutted and narrow, and crossed by a little stream. A nervous horse took fright at the running water, dashed up one of the banks, and firmly embedded the water-cart, which he was pulling, in the other, thus effectively blocking the way.

When the subaltern, having seen everything safe for the night, was returning to report to the major, he found something akin to confusion in the transport. Horses were neighing, backing, plunging, making things worse, as only horses can. If the regiment had been attacked that night, and forced to retire, the way was so completely obstructed that it would probably have been annihilated, as the transport did not get safely away until just before dawn.

He had had no proper food or drink for twenty-four hours, so one can easily imagine how pleased he was to see the major and the captain seated around a table in a little hovel of a cottage, just about to demolish some tea and bread and marmalade.

The air was charged with electricity caused by four men nervously awaiting the boiling of the kettle, and trying to conceal their impatience.

"Poor old —— must have lost himself," said the major, referring to the senior subaltern, "or he'd be here by now; he has a wonderful nose for food."

However, half-way through the meal he came in, admitting that he had lost himself, and wandered into another regiment's lines.

After the meal they returned to their platoons, and spent the usual miserable night in their usual miserable way, cramped by the usual miserable damp. Next morning the regiment was moved further out, to the top of the ridge, to protect the retreat of the remaining two brigades and their transport columns. Luckily the enemy was not in sufficient force to drive this covering party in.

When the division had got clear away, the brigade resumed the column of route formation, and the retreat was continued. Once again during the morning a German *Taube* flew overhead. A violent fusillade broke out from the road, from which the aeroplane suffered less than the men, as they were in too close formation to fire properly. A vast quantity of ammunition was wasted, and the position and strength of the column was thus demonstrated to the airman. It was decided in future to hide as completely as possible, whenever an enemy aeroplane hove in sight, and not on any account to fire at it.

Later on a German patrol menaced the column, but, having forced it to deploy in some measure, withdrew. The rest of the march passed uneventfully, but the country became less flat than hitherto—an addition to their trials!

He tried his French on the battalion's interpreter, who in peace time had been an Avocat in Paris, and who told him many things of the French Army. He spoke of its dauntless patriotism, its passionate longing for revenge, fostered for many long years of national subservience; the determination to avenge the humiliations of Delcassé, of Agadir, of the coronation at Versailles. As vivacious and eloquent as only one of his nation and calling can be, he praised the confidence of the French Army and its "*Généralissime.*" He repeated the great names of the army—De Castlenau, Percin, Sarrail, and many more unknown to the subaltern. He spoke with deep feeling. A spark of the fire that, in her hours of need, never fails his country, had descended upon him, and, in the eyes of the stolid British soldiers around, transformed him.

CHAPTER 8

St. Quentin and La Fère

In the afternoon a large town was reached, probably St. Quentin, through which long trains of motor transport were rumbling. A halt was made some miles to the south of this town. While they were taking their evening meal the ever-pursuing sound of artillery fire was heard from over the ridge. Two of the companies were hastily fallen in, and marched away to this scene of activities, to undergo probably yet another rear-guard action. The remaining companies were then set to dig themselves in, astride the road.

As you have seen from these rough descriptions of the first three days of the battle in Belgium, the most that is seen of the enemy is but a passing glimpse. If the higher command decide that to give battle in any determined measure would be to expose their force to unnecessary chances of defeat, and to endanger the ultimate success of the campaign, it is very unlikely that the infantry soldier will see his enemy at a distance of less than five or six hundred yards. There is always the danger, if the enemy are allowed to come to close quarters, that the defenders will find themselves so pinned to their ground that it is impossible to extricate themselves from their position without losses of greater magnitude than would be warranted by the success obtained. So far this division, at any rate, had succeeded in their mission of delaying the enemy by forcing him to deploy, at the same time taking the greatest care to refuse open battle.

Most of the younger subalterns had very primitive ideas on the general strategy of the campaign. There would be a wait, they thought, as the English Army would probably be used as general reserve; then there would be "the devil of a battle," ending in victory or defeat, and followed by a glorious life (or death), and that would be the end of the matter. It would be over by Christmas, "easy." The actual course of events was very different. The English had encountered the enemy in the first onslaught of battle, and there had been neither victory nor defeat—nothing but retreat, retreat, retreat, over twenty miles a day, in the blazing heat of sunny France, with the fear of capture for those who lagged behind. . . .

The fighting was not like those battles on Laffans Plain, where you fought quickly and decisively, and where, "win, draw, or lose," you were home in time for tea. You were told all about it beforehand by the colonel, or brigadier, and sometimes the "show" approached interest. Here everything was different. This was the real thing. Yet there seemed less reality in it than in the mock battles of Aldershot, with their mock situations, tired charges and rattling bolts. Here you knew nothing, you were barely told where to move. There were none of those charming little papers headed: "*General Idea, White Army moving on*, etc. . . ." and: "*Special Idea, the nth Infantry Brigade, commanded by*, etc. etc. . . ." The "General Idea" of this campaign remained absolute darkness; and already pessimists began to fear that Christmas would not see them back at home.

As far as eagerness to meet the enemy was concerned the "morale" was as high as ever, but nevertheless the temper of the troops was beginning to be badly shaken. They did not understand the necessity for retreat; for not a word had been whispered of other set-backs. They had a ridiculous, but nevertheless firmly lodged, impression that this prolonged retreat was just another of those needless "fatigues" to which they were so often put, and vaguely they resented it, distrusted the necessity for it. Mr. Thomas Atkins found it difficult to believe in the existence of Germans whom he could not see. In a word, he was beginning to be "fed up"; especially the reservists, oldish men who had been called from their homes, bundled once more into uniforms, hurried to a foreign land of which they knew nothing, and pushed into a battle which showed great promise of becoming a "*débacle.*"

But you must not blame the men for this. You must remember that they had left England before the spirit of patriotism had been rekindled. They felt, and before reams of paper had been scattered broadcast to prove the contrary the feeling was very prevalent, that great diplomatic blunders must have been made for the situation to have reached such an impasse. Germany had been out for war before: witness Agadir and similar disturbances in the diplomatic world which occurred with almost monotonous regularity every August. Previously war had simply been denied to Germany. Why not once again? And so on, and so forth. Probably they did not really believe or mean half they said. They were thirsty, hungry, and very, very tired.

The soldier at Malplâquet shook the powder from his wig, and grumbled as only a soldier and a Britain can.

His descendant at Mons did just the same thing. And after he had got his "grouse" off his chest, fought all the better for it.

Although an alarming rumour reached them that the enemy, crowded into motor buses, had already reached St. Quentin, nothing disturbed their rest during the night, and by dawn the column was swinging along the road to La Fère. The men were always depressed and weary in the early morning. Their spirits never began to rise until eight or nine o'clock. Then songs would break out. "Who were you with last night?" "Hold your hand out, naughty boy!" and the inevitable "Tipperary," were the favourites. They would often whistle the "*Marseillaise*." A certain "swing" entered into the marching; there was less changing step, less shuffling. Even their weary faces brightened. Jokes became positively prolific, and the wit of the barrack-room, considered as wit, is far funnier than the humour of the mess. Perhaps it is founded on a deeper knowledge of life.

Towards midday, almost imperceptibly, the gist of the songs changed to the sentimental, and before very long the heat and fatigue gradually overcame the men, and songs ceased altogether. As a general rule, after two o'clock the mental attitude of the troops might be described as black, distinctly black.

The rumour ran down the column that La Fère was to be the termination of that day's march, and as La Fère was only a matter of ten miles away, it was felt that at last an "easy" day had arrived. The road led through very pleasant places along a river valley, the opposite slope of which was wooded. That morning, too, there was no suspicion of artillery fire. It seemed that, for the moment at any rate, they had escaped the inconvenience of battle. Somebody said that La Fère was fortified. Behind its works they would doubtless stand, rest, and then perhaps fight. (Even yet they had not learnt the futility of speculation.)

Those ten miles were long ones. It almost seemed to their tantalised nerves that La Fère was not a town, but a mirage. And so it was, or at least their thoughts of rest and water and food remained "*in nebulis*."

Outside the town was a road-crossing. One way led to the main street of the town, and the other way to the south. To the consternation and amazement of everybody, the khaki ribbon crept, not towards the houses, but seemed for a dreadful moment to hesitate, to wobble, then turned its head slowly and irrevocably away from the town. The men swore. They felt that they were a scale on the skin of a long, sombre, khaki serpent, whose head had acted contrary to the wishes of its belly. And the body of the serpent quivered with indignation. The subaltern himself felt that he had been cheated, lured on by false pretences, and generally treated shamefully. He knew perfectly well that these ideas were groundless and absurd. He knew that the halt at La Fère was only rumour; he knew long marches were the only thing to save them, but in spite of this knowledge he was angry, enraged.

The blood flew still more to his burning cheeks, his teeth snapped together. If he could, he would have flown to the head of the column, drawn his revolver, and emptied it in the face of that general. He positively enjoyed picturing the results of such a crime. He chortled over the idea of the plump figure falling from the comfortable saddle to the hard, hot road. He imagined the neat red cap lying in the grey dust. And his boots, he knew what they would be like—glossy mahogany! Why should anyone have shining boots, when his own were dull and bursting? Why should anyone be clean and shaven when his own face was smeared with dirt and stubble? He exulted inwardly at the thought of the death and mutilation of someone who had never done him the slightest harm, and whose efficiency had probably saved his life.

Such is human nature!

CHAPTER 9

Sir John French

A few miles south of La Fère, the brigade was halted in an orchard for its midday rest. Taking from his pockets the various parts of his safety razor, the subaltern screwed them together, and with the help of a bit of soap, from which the biscuit crumbs and chocolate dust of his haversack had first to be carefully scraped, he shaved. As he was returning, lovingly fingering his once more smooth cheeks, he saw three large Daimler limousines draw up opposite the lines, and recognised them immediately as the authorised pattern of car for the use of the higher British generals in the field.

An officer hurriedly got out, and held open the door with great deference, while a second alighted. The subaltern easily recognised both. The first was the chief of the general staff—Sir Archibald Murray. He was a figure of middle height, with a slight stoop, and slow movements. His face was kindly, mobile—not at all the conventional military face. The mouth was tight shut, as if to suppress all the little humours and witticisms that teemed in the quick blue eyes.

The other figure, short and dapper in build, quick and nervous in motion, need not be described. The blue eyes, the pink skin and white hair of the field-marshal commanding-in-chief are known wherever our language is spoken.

Two of the colonels came forward and saluted as only a senior officer can. A private salutes like a machine; a subaltern is awkward, but a senior officer manages somehow to insinuate into this simple movement deference and admiration, backed, as it were, with determination and self-reliance.

It is as if he were to say: "I have the greatest esteem for you as a great man. I admire your brain and breeding, and will execute your commands with the precision and promptitude that they deserve. But in a lesser sort of way I am just the same, a great man; do not forget it!"

And in response the salute of the great man seems to say: "I heartily appreciate the deference which you have shown me, and honour it the more as it comes from such a man as you." Like the bow of a Versailles courtier, it has its finer points, and is not to be learnt either soon or easily.

The men were called round without any formality, and Sir John French began immediately to address them. It was not the first time that the subaltern had heard him speak. As chief of the imperial general staff, he used to inspect and address the cadets of the Royal Military College, Sandhurst, at the end of each term. And he did it well. The subaltern remembered the sight of the long parade—"three sides of a square" the formation was called—and the generals with the skirts of their "frock" coats and the feathers in their hats blowing in the wind. But in spite of the absence of red coats, and the stiffness of parade, this was a more moving harangue than any he had heard on the parade ground at Sandhurst.

The field-marshal said that the greatest battle that had ever been fought was just over. It had rolled with the fury of a cyclone from Belfort to Mons. Nearly two million men had been engaged, and the British Army had emerged from the contest covered with glory, having for three days maintained an unbroken front in the face of an overwhelming superiority in numbers. Never had he been more proud to be a British soldier than he was that day. The regiment had added yet another branch to its laurel wreath. It had more than sustained its ancient traditions for endurance and courage. He was proud of it.

The enemy had been nearly five to one, and yet had been unable to inflict defeat upon them. If they had been "broken," the whole of the French left would have assuredly perished. Thanks to their endurance and obedience in the face of great provocation and privation, the Allied armies were now free from the dangers that had threatened them. No one knew better than he did that they would continue to be as brave, as reliable, and as soldierly in the future, as they had been in the past, until final victory had been fully accomplished! . . .

How they cheered him as he made his way to his car!

At first the Tommies had not realised what was happening. There had been disturbing cries of "What's all this abart?" "Oo's the 'ole bloke?" But they had soon ceased, and in a few seconds the men were crowding round with eager faces, hanging on the words of their leader. He commiserated with them upon their losses; he understood what they had been through. In a word, he appreciated them, and in the army appreciation is a "rare and refreshing fruit." Although they would have died rather than own it, there was a feeling of tears behind the eyes of a good many of those tough old warriors. The personality of the field-marshal, and his heartening words, had brightened many a grim face, and lightened many a heavy load.

CHAPTER 10

A Pause, and More Marching

A village called Amigny was reached at about six o'clock in the evening, and here the battalion, in its usual evening state of prostration, was billeted.

The company settled down in the chief "*estaminet*" of the place. The decision was a faulty one. The old woman who was hostess gave way to hysterics at the thought of having to provide for five large, hungry and nervous officers. She was a horrid old woman—mean, dirty, and if the captain's word could be taken as strict truth, immoral. Still, a roof to cover their heads was an unusual blessing, and it was not long before they were all sound asleep.

Next morning there was no parade in the grey of dawn. As the first chilly beam of light crept into the room the subaltern turned in his sleep, and smiled at the complete luxury of prolonged rest. They did not get up till eight, and having dressed, washed, and even shaved, they had what the "hostess" called breakfast. And still nothing happened, no breathless orderly delivered the usual order. What had happened?

The senior subaltern, who was suspected of leanings towards matrimony, began to write a letter.

The captain, who was energetic, began to play billiards on the miniature pocketless table. Later on the colonel came in. It was not an official visit, only to warn them to be ready to move at any moment. Having thanked the old woman, he left in a singularly peaceful frame of mind.

At half-past twelve they moved on to a small hill just outside the village, which they proceeded to put into a state of defence. They heard that afternoon of a large counter-attack launched in the neighbourhood of Guise, which had been successful in temporarily relieving the pressure on the British front. Here it was that they first heard rumours of the affair off Heligoland, which had become inflated into a tremendous victory for the British fleet. Apparently half the German Fleet had been sent to the bottom of the sea, and you can imagine the state of enthusiasm that was caused by this news. They felt that, no matter what might happen to them on the battlefields of France, their homes at any rate were freed from the menace of the German. To add to their jubilation, instead of having to spend the night in the trenches they had dug, they were marched back, for some inexplicable reason, to their billets in the village.

Next morning they paraded as soon as it was light, and the retreat was continued throughout the day.

There was a very marked change in the country. The open cornfields were replaced by woods of such a dense nature that any operations would have been impossible. Curious as it may seem, the Subaltern had in some way been upset by the previous day's break in the usual marching routine. The heat seemed more intense than ever; his haversack and equipment more cumbersome. But the roads were now avenues, and the overhanging branches provided very welcome shade.

They emerged from the woods, once more to strike out in the glaring sunlight. Soon a hill was seen in the distance, surmounted by a quaint and squat tower, very reminiscent of Windsor. The houses which clustered beneath it formed the little town of Coucy-le-Chateau. They camped out in an open field beneath the hill, and by stripping a couple of haystacks made themselves fairly comfortable. They must have very effectually shaken off the enemy, for the general did not think it necessary to put out outposts.

The next morning, this time well before dawn, the retreat was continued, apparently on Soissons. Precisely the same thing happened on this day as on the march to La Fère. Soissons was no great distance from Coucy, only some eight or ten miles, and just when they reached the northern heights of the Aisne, and the whole town was visible, the brigade sheered off to the right, and clung to the river bank.

Soissons looked so particularly inviting, the whites and greys and primroses of its walls flashing in the sun. The sight of a French town (in the distance) is very pleasing to any one used to the terra-cotta reds of England. The cobbles give the streets such a medieval air, the green shutters seem so queer, and there is such a disdain of geometry. But when one gets right into the town, a violent change comes over the scene. The cobbles that were so pleasantly medieval in the distance become, under one's feet, nothing but an ankle-turning plague. The stuccoed walls look very clean in the distance, but near to, the filth of the streets modifies one's admiration. A small French town generally reminds one of the outhouses and styes of a farm. The air is diffuse with the scent of manure. England, with all thy drainage system, I love thee still!

The road now clung to the river, which was not actually crossed until two or three o'clock in the afternoon. The bridge was a large and substantial structure, and a section of engineers were preparing to blow it up. Before the hour's halt was over, the inevitable alarm occurred, and two companies were detached to fight the usual rearguard action, under the major, who was now second-in-command.

The remainder of the battalion continued the march, this time along the south bank of the river.

The heat was as usual intense, and today they missed the shady trees that had so well protected them the day before. A couple of hours later they turned abruptly to the left, that is to say, southwards, and the Aisne disappeared in a cleft of the hills. Winding tortuously at the feet of more or less steep slopes—for the country was quite changed—progress was not as easy as it had been. At last, close on seven o'clock, a halt was made on a hillside.

Men fell to the ground with a grunt, thanking God that another of those Hell-days was over. Too tired to move, even if the position was an uncomfortable one; too tired to pray for rest; too tired to think!

The average man is, I am sure, quite ignorant of the effect which extreme exhaustion has on the brain. As the weary hours drag by, it seems as if a deadness, a sort of paralysis, creeps up the limbs, upwards towards the head. The bones of the feet ache with a very positive pain. It needs a concentration of mind that a stupefied brain can ill afford to give to force the knees to keep from doubling under the weight of the body. The hands feel as if they were swelling until the boiling blood would ooze from the finger-tips. The lungs seem too exhausted to expand; the neck too weary to support the heavy head. The shoulders ache under the galling weight of sword and haversack, and every inch of clammy skin on the body seems ten times as sensitive as it normally is. The nerves in the face and hands feel like swelled veins that itch so that they long to be torn by the nails. The tongue and eyes seem to expand to twice their usual size. Sound itself loses its sharp conciseness, and reaches the brain only as a blurred and indistinct impression.

But perhaps the reader may say that he has once done twenty-five or thirty miles in a day, and did not feel half as bad as that. He must remember, however, that these men had been doing over twenty-five miles every day for the last ten days, and that, in addition to the physical fatigue, they had suffered the mental fatigue caused by fighting. Their few hours of halting were generally occupied by trench digging. They were not having a fifth of the sleep that such a life requires. They were protected neither from the heat of noon nor from the chill of dawn. The food they got was not fresh food, and their equipment weighed ninety pounds! Lesser men would have died; men imbued with a feebler determination would have fainted.

As it was, the transport was crowded with men whose feet had failed them, and many must have fallen behind, to be killed or made prisoner. The majority "stuck it" manfully, and faced every fresh effort with a cool, gruff determination that was wonderful. This spirit saved the Allies from the first frenzied blow of Germany, in just the same way that it had saved England from the Armada and from Napoleon.

The subaltern realised the value of his men; indeed, he felt a wholesome trust and faith in them that individual outbursts of bad temper or lack of discipline could not shake. They occupied, more than they had ever done before, the greater part of his thoughts and attention. He made their safety and comfort his first care, and protected them from ridiculous orders and unnecessary fatigue. He found himself watching and playing upon their moods. He tried very hard and earnestly to make them a good officer. He thought that they were the salt of the earth, that there never had been men like them, nor would be again.

No sooner had a scanty meal been rammed down their throats than they were paraded once more, and hurried away to the crest of another ridge. One of the Aisne bridges had been left standing, and apparently the enemy was across it, and already threatening to envelop their position. Having reached higher ground they stopped for what was left of the night, since it was impossible for the enemy cavalry to attack them in that country.

CHAPTER 11

A Rear-Guard Action

In a couple of hours' time the march was continued in the darkness. The men lurched from side to side, with brains too fagged to control their feet. The company was sent out to act as flank-guard on the top of the crest beneath which the column was moving. This movement was very tiresome, as they had to move over broken country in an *extended* formation, and to keep up with the column which was moving in *close* formation along the road. To compensate for this they were able to fill their haversacks with a peculiarly sweet kind of apple.

Later in the morning they emerged from the close country into the typical open plains of France, covered with corn and vegetables. About five or six miles of this, and then the darker greens of pine and fir forests appeared in view.

The general staff had selected this as the site of yet another rear-guard action. One of the other brigades in the division was already busily engaged in constructing a line of trenches not more than a hundred yards in front of the woods. To their front the view was uninterrupted, offering a field of fire unbroken by the least suspicion of cover from view or fire.

The artillery was no doubt concealed in the woods behind. The men were doing their work with a quick, noiseless efficiency that would have made you very proud if you could have seen them.

Soon after the column had passed into the woods, the noise of the guns was heard. The subaltern could imagine the whole scene as vividly as if he could see it: the van-guard of the German advanced guard suddenly "held up" by the bursting of the British shells; the hasty deployment of the German cavalry; the further "holding up" of the main-guard of the advanced guard while a reconnaissance was being carried out with the help, perhaps, of a *"Taube."* Remember that the Germans must have been daily, almost hourly, expecting the Allies to make a determined attempt to check their continued advance, and must have been very nervous of walking into some trap. Therefore the commander of the German advanced guard would have to discover very exactly the nature of the resistance in front of him before the officer commanding the main body—some miles behind, of course—could decide what force it would be necessary to deploy in order to dislodge the enemy from his position.

This is no easy matter. What the retreating army is fighting for is time—time to get clean away. Consequently, if the officer commanding the advancing army deploys a larger force than is necessary, he grants his opponent the very thing that he wants—time, since the deployment of, say, a division is a very lengthy operation, occupying at least three hours. On the other hand, if he details too small a force for the work, his attack is held in check, and more time than ever is wasted in reinforcing it in a measure sufficient to press home the attack.

The subaltern imagined the long wait while the shells shrieked over the heads of the infantry towards an enemy as yet unseen. Then the enemy shells would begin to feel their way to the thin brown line of trenches, and under cover of their fire the infantry, now deployed into fighting formations, would "advance." Then our men would begin firing, firing with cool precision. The landscape would soon be dotted with grey ants. Machine-guns would cut down whole lines of grey ants with their *"plop-plop-plop."* Shrapnel would burst about whole clouds of grey ants, burying them in brown clouds of dust. Finally, the directing brain would decide that it was time to cut and run. The artillery fire would be increased tenfold, and under cover of it the brown ants would scamper from the trenches and disappear into the green depths of the woods.

Soon the firing would cease. The retreating party would have got safely, cleanly away, having gained many precious hours for the main body, and having incidentally inflicted severe losses on the enemy. The latter, have nothing left to do but to re-form (thus losing still more time), would then continue his pursuit weaker and further from his opponent than he had been before.

At last, striking a clearing, the town of Villiers Cotterets was reached. There was nothing to distinguish it from a score of other small agricultural centres through which the column had passed. The only thing the subaltern remembers about this town is that he handed a French peasant woman there a couple of *francs* on the odd chance that she would bring back some chocolate. She did not.

On the further side of the town the brigade transport, with steaming cookers, was massed ready to give the troops a midday meal. This was an innovation greatly appreciated. Such a thing as a meal in the middle of the day had not occurred since the days of Iron.

CHAPTER 12

Villiers-Cotterets

Twenty minutes later the column was again on the move, but this time not for long. Having reached the edge of another forest, a fresh halt was made while the transport was hauled past them into the wood. The transport, known technically as "second line" of a brigade, is a very large, cumbersome, and slow-moving affair, and it must be protected at all costs, for without it the brigade is lost.

A swift deployment was then made, and the edge of the wood was held astride of the road. After everything had been arranged, there was a wait of thirty to forty minutes. Nothing could be seen, as the position was on the "reverse slope" of the incline, but the field of fire was absolutely clear for at least two hundred yards in front. It is the most trying time of all, this waiting for the approach of an enemy you cannot see, and it tells on the most phlegmatic disposition. The men occupy the heavy moments by working the bolts of their rifles, and seeing that they work easily. The success or failure of the defence depends mainly on the speed and accuracy with which the defenders "get their rounds off."

The officers pace about, making sure of "keeping touch" with the units on their flank, discovering the best way to retire, and so on. There is at such moments an odd desire to give way to the temptation of saying to oneself, "Where shall I be in an hour's time?" One gazes with a subtle feeling of affection on one's limbs, and wonders, "Where shall I get it?" Subconsciously one is amused and a little ashamed of such concessions to sentimentality. The best thing to do under the circumstances is to go and check the range-finders' figures, or prepare the headlines of a message or two.

★★★★★★

A *Taube*, like some huge insect with a buzz of whirring wings, flew

47

overhead, dropping multi-coloured stars from its tail. Then our guns "opened the ball."

There was something blatant and repulsive about that first burst of sound. The ferns of the forest shivered, as if awakened from a sunny dream to face terrible calamities. The trees seemed to shake with a delicate fear of what was in store for them. The enemy's fire burst upon them with a startling intensity.

There was no point in holding the advanced edge of the wood under such a bombardment until the actual appearance of the enemy infantry made it necessary, so the whole line was retired some fifty yards into the wood. By this manoeuvre the colonel lost no advantage, and must have saved many lives.

Although artillery fire had been a pretty frequent occurrence, this was the heaviest the men had yet experienced. The noise was ear-splitting; the explosions filled the quivering air; the ground seemed to shudder beneath them. Branches fell crashing to the ground; it seemed as if a god was flogging the tree-tops with a huge scourge. The din was awful, petrifying, numbing.

And in the middle of all this inferno, with the sight of men with ashen faces limping, crawling, or being dragged to the rear, with the leaves on the ground smoking from the hot, jagged shell-casings buried among them, the subaltern suddenly discovered that he was not afraid. The discovery struck him as curious. He argued with himself that he had every right to feel afraid, that he ought to feel "queer." He said to himself, "Here you are, as nervous and temperamental a youth as ever stepped, with a mental laziness that amounts to moral cowardice, in the deuce of a hole that I don't expect you'll ever get out of. You ought to be in an awful state. Your cheeks ought to be white, and there they are looking like two raw beef-steaks. Your tongue ought to cleave to the roof of your mouth; and it isn't. You ought to feel pains in the pit of your stomach, and you're not. Devil a bit! You know, you're missing all the sensations that the writers told you about. You're not playing the game. Come, buck up, fall down and grovel on the ground!" But he did not. He did not want to. He felt absolutely normal.

A man sheltering behind the same tree suddenly spun round, and, grasping his left arm, fell with a thud to the ground. He reeled over, with knees raised and rounded back, and staggered immediately to his feet. "Oh, my arm, my arm!" he moaned plaintively, and turned away towards the rear, whimpering a little as he went, and tenderly holding the wet, dark-stained sleeve as he went. The subaltern felt that he ought to have winced with horror at the mutilation of the poor stricken thing, but beyond a slight sinking sensation between the lungs and the stomach, the incident left him with no emotion. He picked up the man's rifle, leant it against the tree, and continued to scan the skyline with his glasses, feeling all the while a bit of a brute.

At the same time he experienced a sensation of pleasure at the immunity from mental sufferings that are generally supposed to afflict men under these conditions. He felt like a man who unexpectedly finds a five-pound note, the very existence of which he had forgotten, hidden away in some unusual pocket. It was something of the same sensation that he used to have at school, when by chance he saw other boys working at impositions which he had himself escaped.

The time came when it was no longer expedient to remain in the wood, so they advanced, flitting from tree to tree, back to the edge of the forest. The view was rather restricted from where the subaltern was, apparently on the right of where the full force of the attack was breaking.

"*Plop-plop-plop*," the machine-gun spluttered with an amazing air of detached insistence. The machine-guns strike in battle quite a note of their own. Shells, screeching and roaring in their frenzy, give an impression of passion, of untameable wrath. Rifle-fire is as inconstant in volume as piano music; there is something of human effort to be heard in the "*tap . . . tap . . . tap . . . tap-tap-trrrrapp*" of its *crescendos* and *diminuendos*. But the machine-gun is different from these. It strikes a higher note, and can be heard above the roar of the bursting shells. It is mechanical, there is nothing about it of human passion; it is a machine, and a most deadly one at that.

The colonel dashed out into the open and dragged a wounded gunner into the comparative shelter of the wood. Many more acts scarcely less heroic were performed.

At last the moment came to retire. The guns had already rattled through the line, and the companies drew away from the edge of the wood, re-formed with great speed, and were soon marching once more in column of route along the road.

The subaltern felt exhausted in a way that he had never felt so badly before. The withdrawal from the actual scene of battle seemed to leave a gulf in his inside that positively yawned. It was not only the apparent uselessness of trying to stem the German tide that depressed him. There was something more than that. He felt like a man who wakes after a heavy, drug-induced slumber. The sudden cessation of the intense excitement of battles leaves the brain empty and weary. At such moments the hopelessness of the whole thing appalled and depressed him. The uncertainty of the future hurt him. Nor was he alone in this state of mind. Not a voice was raised to break the throbbing monotony of the march. Heads were bent low.

On they went. Night came down upon them and seemed to crush the spirit out of them. As they emerged from the wood, the moon rose and flooded the broad plain with weird, phosphorescent light. They struggled on, swaying with sleep, past the ghostly outlines of poplars and hayricks, past quiet, deserted cottages and empty stables. There was something almost unearthly about that march in the moonlight. The accumulated fatigue of a long and hot day, the want of food and the repressing influence of a summer night, all these things joined in producing a state of mental listlessness that destroyed the impression of reality which things have in the daytime. They were drifting down a slow-moving stream; the scenery glided by, but the sensation was by no means pleasant.

The brain was constantly at war with the lazy feet, striving to keep them from stumbling and the eyelids from closing. Sound was peculiarly muffled, as if darkness repressed and shut it in. The brain was not commanding the limbs with the instantaneous co-ordination of the daytime. The sensation that this produced—it is very difficult to give any definite idea of it—was an impression of physical and mental incompetence and uncertainty. And all the time every ounce of the body was crying out to the mind to let it lie down and rest.

That night many men were lost.

★★★★★★

It was not until ten o'clock that they arrived at a village where they found the "cookers" and regimental transport. The subaltern could not help admiring the skill which was constantly being shown by the staff not only in the strategical dispositions of the retreat, but in comparatively minute details such as this. The brigade transport had been guided and collected to a spot where it could safely be of service to the battalions. Moreover, when the men arrived they found tea waiting for them already brewed. Apparently the hour of the men's arrival had been timed to such a nicety that the meal was just ready for them. Assuming the truth of Napoleon's maxim about an army marching on its belly, one can easily see from these pages that if staff work had in any way failed, or if the Army Service Corps had broken down, the Great Retreat would have ended in disaster. It was these faultless arrangements of the Army Service Corps that served to keep the sorely tried army at any rate on its legs.

A fire had been lighted, and, grateful for its warmth, the five officers of the company were soon clustering round it, sipping out of their mess tins filled with strong, sweet tea, without milk but very strongly flavoured with rum. Soon the worries and painful memories of the day were dispelled. A feeling almost of contentment stole over them. There is something so particularly adventurous and at the same time soothing about a camp fire. They had all read books at school full of camp fires and fighting and prairies, and they had all more or less envied such a life. Here it was. But the adventure part of it was so minute, and the drudgery and nerve strain so great that the most adventurous soul among them had long since admitted that "if *this* was active service, it was not the life for him!"

CHAPTER 13

Heat and Dust

The subaltern did not get to sleep until twelve, and the regiment made another start as early as half-past two. It seemed to him that when necessity drives there is no limit to the nerve force that we have in us! They marched some miles in a westerly direction before they rejoined the main road southwards.

To describe in detail the sufferings of that day would be to repeat almost word for word some of the preceding paragraphs. It was just as hot as usual, just as dusty as usual. An order had come from somewhere that there was to be no looting. Men were to be forbidden to snatch an apple from a fruit-strewn orchard, or an egg from a deserted barn! The owners had already fled from their homes, and here Mr. Thomas Atkins was solemnly asked to go hungry and thirsty and to relieve the enemy of one of his greatest difficulties—feeding himself. The platoon having halted for the usual hourly halt outside an orchard, some of the men broke into it and began to throw apples over the hedge to the others. Seeing the colonel approaching, the subaltern realised that something must be done instantly to avert disaster. "What the deuce are you men doing? Come out of it!" he cried. The men came, looking very dejected. The colonel, pacified, passed by. A second later, the glad work of refreshing the troops was being carried on by a fresh couple of men.

It must have been a very similar situation that gave birth to a story that has already become famous. A Tommy was caught by a "brass hat" in the very act of strangling a chicken. Tommy looked up. Was he abashed? Not a bit of it! He did what Mr. Thomas Atkins generally does in a tight corner. He kept his head: he rose magnificently to the occasion. He did not loose the chicken and endeavour to stammer an apology. On the contrary, he continued to strangle it. He took no notice of the "brass hat." As he gave a final twist to the bird's throat he said menacingly, "So you'd try to bite me, would you, you little brute!"

Towards the end of the afternoon the men were so obviously exhausted, and the number forced to fall out was so great, that a halt had to be ordered in spite of previous plans. The men threw themselves utterly exhausted on the ground on their backs, and lay like so many corpses until the march was continued, in the cool of the evening.

The subaltern, consulting a fresh map—for they had been walking across the ground covered by one map every day—learnt to his surprise that they were within a few miles of Paris. And so also, he thought, were the Germans! It rather looked as if they were heading straight towards the city, and that would mean a siege. It was no use worrying about things, but that depressing idea was in the minds of most of the officers that evening. Not that the subaltern cared much at the time—it would mean a stop to this everlasting marching, and perhaps the forts of Paris could stand it; anyhow the German fleet had been rounded up. (That wicked rumour spread by the sensational section of the press had not yet been denied.)

While he was thinking of these things, they were moving through a country far more thickly populated. Villages began to crowd upon each other's heels, and all the villages—cheering sight—were full of British soldiers settling down to their billets for the night. This was the first they had seen of any other division except their own, and the sight rather dispelled the illusion that, for all these days, they had been alone and unaided in a land of "frightfulness."

More marching in the darkness!

At last, at about nine o'clock, they reached their billets, but the word scarcely conveys a correct impression of the palatial *château* in which they were quartered. There was considerable delay in settling the men (which must, of course, be done before an officer thinks of his own comfort) and in detailing the quarters. At length the officers of the company found themselves in a little bedroom overlooking a river which they supposed to be the Seine. The captain, who had been sent on in front of the battalion to allot billets, produced with pride some chocolate, sardines, and bottled mushrooms.

The second lieutenants went in search of the "company cookers" to "draw" their tea (in a washing jug), while the senior subaltern effected a felonious entry into the room allotted to the general, and purloined all the drinking glasses he could lay hands on, making his departure just as that worthy officer was coming up the stairs.

The house was evidently of the "*nouveau riche*" type. If there was in it nothing that could actually offend the eye, there was certainly nothing to satisfy it. There was a profusion of gilt mirrors, and an aching lack of pictures: the lighting was too new and glaring: the upholstery too flimsy. But there were baths and soap! It was too late for the baths, but the soap quickly disappeared.

Just when they were settling themselves drowsily to enjoy a real sleep, free from the fear of a morning attack, protected from the damp of dawn, and with quilts of down to cover them, who should come in but the colonel!

CHAPTER 14

The Occupation of Villiers

"I'm sorry," he said, "but we've got to parade at two in the morning."

As soon as the door had closed behind him a perfect volley of abuse was heard. They could not dismiss from their minds the thought that all this sort of thing was unnecessary. And this was very natural, as no one had had sufficient courage to tell the regimental officer how serious the position was.

Even two hours' sleep, however, is better than none.

As soon as it became light the subaltern saw that they were counter-marching along the same road on which they had travelled the previous night. What did this mean? Was a stand going to be made at last? Apparently not, for the resting-place of last afternoon was passed, and they continued to move eastwards. On consulting the map, he judged that they were marching on Meaux on the Aisne. He had often read of Meaux; was it not the Bishopric of Bossuet, the stately orator of Louis XIV? The interest he felt in the question helped to take the weight from his weary limbs.

At last they crossed the bridge. Sappers had been at work on it for some time, and the preparations to blow it up after they had passed were almost complete. The first sight of interest was the railway station, which was filled with what appeared to the subaltern to be double-decked trains. Evidently a French army had detrained here.

The column swung suddenly round a corner and they were almost staggered with the sight of the cathedral towering above them. To an eye used exclusively to the sight of the dour British edifice, there is something very fascinating about a foreign cathedral such as this. There is something more daring about the style of architecture, something more flamboyant, and yet more solid. The cathedral seemed vaguely indicative of the past grandeur of the Catholic Church. Bathed in the early morning sunlight it appeared to exult over the mean smallness of the houses that clustered at its feet.

Beyond the cathedral there is nothing at all extraordinary about Meaux. Many months afterwards one of his nurses told him in hospital that she had spent a long time in that very street. She had been with her father, the erstwhile colonel of a line regiment, and a specialist in strategy, who for the pure love of the thing had laboriously gained permission to stay at Meaux and visit the famous battlefields of the Marne. She said they had been in the very room where General Joffre met Field-Marshal French, and had bought the very teapot in which their tea was brewed. She rather wondered how many more of these "very" teapots had been sold at fancy prices!

If Von Kluck made a forward thrust at Paris before his sidelong movement to the south-east, it was undoubtedly made at Meaux, which was the scene of some terrific combats.

Emerging from the town, the column branched off in a south-easterly direction, and ascended the sides of a very steep plateau. Having reached the flat ground at the top, a midday halt was made in the pleasant grounds of yet another *château*.

This fresh move was discussed a great deal as the men lay at full length in the shade of the trees. Evidently there was to be no siege of Paris. They were marching directly away from Paris. What did it mean? They would get to Marseilles in a fortnight at this rate, and then the only thing to do would be to wire for the fleet, and be taken safely home to their mammas!

The march went on through the stifling heat of the afternoon, and the subaltern knew that he, and most of the men as well, were feeling about as bad as it is possible to feel without fainting. They marched through a very dense wood, and then out once more into the open. Even the longest day has its ending, and at last they found themselves halted in the usual lines of companies in the usual stubble field. A *Taube* flew overhead and all sorts of fire were concentrated on it.

It was already sunset. After the edge, as it were, had been taken off his exhaustion, the subaltern extracted the before-mentioned piece of soap, and having, as usual, scraped it ready for action, washed his feet in a little stream. He did it under the impression that marching for that day was over. It is very comfortable to wash your hot, tired feet in a cool stream provided there is no necessity to put your boots on again. If something happens that forces you to do this, you are in for a hard and painful job. You would not believe it possible for feet to swell like yours have swelled. They do not seem like your own feet at all. They have expanded past recognition, and their tenderness surpasses thought.

The subaltern was sitting by the stream edge gazing at the flush of golden light in the west, when he was awakened by the major.

"Well, young feller, I've been looking everywhere for you. You've got to take your platoon out to this village, Villiers, and occupy it till further orders—a sort of outpost position—you will be too far from the main body to establish touch; you have really just to block the roads, and if you are rushed, retire here the best way you can."

Having made sure of the position on the map, and asked for a couple of cyclists to accompany him, the subaltern began to put on his boots. But they would not go on. It was like trying to get a baby's boots on to a giant's feet, and the more he tugged the more it hurt. The precious moments of daylight would soon be gone, and in the dark it would be ten times more difficult to find the village and block the roads. There was nothing for it but to cut the boots, so, unwrapping a fresh Gillette blade, he made a large V-shaped gash in the top part of each. It was annoying to have to spoil good boots, and in addition his feet would get wet far sooner than hitherto.

All superfluous articles of weight had long since been thrown away, and consequently he had nothing except matches with which to read his map in the dark and windy night. The difficulty was increased by the fact that the way lay across small tracks which were almost impossible to distinguish, but eventually, more by luck than judgment, he brought his men into a village. Was it Villiers? It took him some time to find out. There were plenty of people in the village street, but the subaltern could not get coherent speech out of any one of them. Fear makes an uneducated Englishman suspicious, quickwitted and surly. It drives the French peasant absolutely mad. That village street seemed to have less sense, less fortitude, less coolness than a duck-run invaded by a terrier. The subaltern caught a man by the arm and pushed him into a doorway.

"*Qu'est-ce que c'est, le nom de cette village?*" he said, with as much insistence and coolness as he could muster. The poor fellow broke into a tirade in which his desire to cut German throats, his peculiarly unfortunate circumstances, and his wish to get away literally tripped over each other.

"*Qu'est-ce que c'est, le nom de cette village?*" Followed a flood of words apparently about the village. A third time. *"Qu'est-ce que c'est, le nom de cette village?"* At last: "Ah, *M'sieur*, Villiers," with an air of surprise, as if he thought the subaltern had known all the time, and had asked merely to start a polite conversation.

He let the man go, and turned his attention to the village street, which presented a terrible spectacle of panic. It was obviously unwise to allow this mob to leave the village, as they seemed to wish, and disperse, shouting and shrieking, over the countryside. Very possibly there were spies amongst them, who would bring the enemy about his ears in half an hour. More likely still, the whole excited crowd would wander straight into the arms of the Germans, and be treated with the well-known restraint of Huns towards the unprotected. So he hurriedly placed guards at the chief outlets of the village, with orders, in addition to the usual duties towards the enemy, to prevent the French from leaving it.

He then returned and tried to pacify the inhabitants. But his kind, soothing words in execrable French did not succeed in dispelling the panic and fear. He had to draw his sword (for the purpose of intimidation only) and literally to thrust them into houses. And he had to get three men with fixed bayonets to help him. He did his best to make it generally understood that anyone who came out of his house and made a noise would be summarily disposed of. Any sounds of confusion would inevitably have drawn the fatal attentions of the enemy.

He then made a hurried survey of the roads leading out of the village, placed sentry groups at various places of advantage, and established the picket in the centre of the village in a large barn. This done, he sent the cyclist orderly to try and get into touch with the village on the right, which, he had been told, was to be occupied by a platoon from another regiment. The cyclist returned to report that the village was deserted by the French, and that there was no sign of the Blankshires. Evidently the O.C. platoon had not been so fortunate in finding his way in the dark.

Dawn broke, and the expected order to retire did not come. The men slept on, intent on snatching as many moments of precious sleep as possible.

Still no orders came. At about eight o'clock the subaltern finally awoke, and went the rounds of his groups. There was nothing to report, all had been quiet.

When he got back he found that the men had collected quite a good number of eggs from abandoned farmyards, had lighted a fire, and were busy making a sort of stew out of bully beef and swedes, and (he strongly suspected) a stolen chicken. As no orders came still, when he had finished his breakfast, he lay down in the shade of an apple tree and continued his sleep. He woke up later, at about midday, and ate the remainder of his rations, and then fell asleep once more.

★★★★★★

He was awakened by the major. It was about four o'clock, and the remainder of the brigade was already on the move. The posts guarding the roads were hastily drawn in, and his platoon took its place in the company as the battalion marched by.

He felt extremely pleased with the whole adventure of Villiers. It was the first and only time that he had had a completely detached command. He had felt the intoxication of undisputed authority; there had been a subtle pleasure in the thought that, as far as help or supervision were concerned, he was absolutely alone and that the responsibility for anything that might happen hung exclusively on his shoulders. The whole day had seemed like a Sunday to him—the first real Sunday since ages and ages ago he had left England, the easy land of peace.

There had been an air of quietness about that afternoon which is peculiar to Sundays, and he congratulated himself on the hours of sleep that he had been able to put in.

From his own point of view the whole war began to seem like an organised campaign of things in general to hustle him about in the heat until he died from want of sleep!

CHAPTER 15

The Last Lap

On every side the results of long marches were only too plain. Spirits were damped. There were fewer songs, and no jokes. The men were not by any means "downhearted," and would rather have died than admit that they were depressed, but the brightness was all rubbed off, and a moroseness, a dense, too-tired-to-worry taciturnity had set in that was almost bullet-proof.

Although the familiar sounds of artillery boomed away quite close to them they were not deployed, and when it was dark they bivouacked along the side of the road.

That night the colonel addressed the officers at some length. "The old man" always had an impressive way of speaking, and darkness and overwrought nerves doubtless magnified this. He spoke in subdued tones, as if awed by the intense silence of the night.

We all could tell where we were, he said—a few miles east, or even south-east by east of the French capital. Our base, Havre, lay to the north-west, with the enemy in between. It was unnecessary to say anything further. The facts spoke for themselves. The British Army was up against it, none could tell what would happen next. One duty, however, was self-evident, and that was to watch the food-supply.

Things were going to be serious. Henceforward the army was to be on half rations, and he knew what that meant. He had been on "half rations" in the South African war, and he had seen a man give a franc for a dirty biscuit, and he knew what it was for soldiers on active service to be hungry. He ordered us, he begged and prayed them, to spare no energy in stopping waste of any description, and making their men realise the gravity of the position. No officer was in future to draw any rations from the company cookers, and the mess sergeant had somehow procured and victualed a mess-cart.

That night must have been the most fateful night in the history of France. All the world was watching with bated breath, watching to see whether France was really a "back number"—whether the Prussian was truly the salt of the earth. If Paris fell, the French armies in the field were cut off from their base; defeat was certain, and the national history of France, or, at any rate, the glory of it, would be stamped out for ever under the *Kaiser's* heel. The fate of France was in the balance, and also the fate of the Russian armies. If Paris fell, Europe might be as much the slave of Prussia as it had been a century ago of Napoleon. As for England, if her fleet could master the German, well and good. But, if not. . . .

It looked as if the enemy were within an ace of victory. He had flooded Belgium and Luxembourg with his armies, and, at the first clash of arms, had hurled everything before him in a manner which to the civilian must have appeared terrible in its completeness. Several times had the defenders apparently attempted to stand, and as many times had they been hurled with even greater violence southwards. And now, before the campaign was a month old, the enemy were within an ace of the most complete victory of modern times. Many men will never forget that night—men on either side with high commands.

How the *Kaiser* must have chuckled when the French Cabinet left for Bordeaux! Bombastic phrases were perchance chasing themselves through his perverted mind. How fine he would look at Versailles, strutting about the Hall of Victories. He would sleep in the bed of the "*Grand Monarque*"—and in Les Invalides how he would smile at the tomb of Napoleon! Perhaps his statesmen were that very night drafting the terms of peace that a crushed adversary would be only too thankful to accept. His day had come at last! Henceforward how he would laugh at democracy and socialism. He would show them that he was master. The best weapon in all the world was sudden, bloody war. He would show his people that he was their Master, their Salvation, their War Lord. He was the greatest man in history, so he thought that night.

There may come a time when he will realise that, after all, he was only the most contemptible and pitiable. But that is by the way.

His generals could not have been so sure. They must have seen the exhaustion of their men. Von Kluck must have already felt the weight of the army, rushed out of Paris by General Galliéni, that threatened to envelop his right flank. Von Heeringen must have realised that the offensive was being wrenched from his grasp. And the crown prince was throwing himself in vain upon the forts of Verdun and Nancy.

That night, too, somewhere behind the French lines, a man of very different stamp from the *Kaiser* was putting the final touches to the preparations of the greatest counter-attack in history. He knew that the enemy had literally overstepped his lines of communications, was exhausted, and nervous of failure so far from his bases. He knew that as long as de Castelnau clung on to the heights around Verdun, his centre and left were safely hinged upon a fortress under cover of which he could launch his counter-offensive with all the weight of his now completely mobilised reinforcements. Moreover, the army that had hurried pell-mell from Paris in taxicabs, in carts, in any form of conveyance that the authorities could lay hands upon, was now completely established on the left of the British, and if Von Kluck, lured on by the prize of Paris, pushed on, he would be outnumbered on his front and very seriously menaced on his right, and disaster would be certain.

Not that the subaltern knew or cared much for these things. He and his men were past caring. Continuous retreat had first evoked surprise, then resentment, then, as fatigue began to grip them like a vice, a kind of dull apathy. He felt he would not have cared whatever happened. The finer emotions of sorrow or hope or happiness were drugged to insensibility. With the exception of odd moments when, absolutely causelessly, wild anger and ungovernable rage took possession of him and seemed to make his blood boil and seethe, he seemed to be degenerating into the state of mind commonly attributed to the dumb beasts of the field—indifferent to everything in the wide world except food and sleep.

That night a draft commanded by one subaltern arrived to fill up the gaps.

The next day the retreat continued. The men's nerves were tried to breaking-point, and a little detail, small and of no consequence in itself, opened the lock, as it were, to a perfect river of growing anger and discontent.

This was how it happened. The colonel had repeated the previous night the order about looting, and the men were under the impression that if any of them took so much as a green apple he would be liable to "death or some such less punishment as the act shall provide." They talk about it and grumble, and then suddenly, without any warning except a clucking and scratching, the mess sergeant is seen by the greater part of the battalion to issue triumphantly from a farm gate with two or three fat hens under his arms. Smiling broadly, totally ignorant of the enormity of his conduct, he deposits his load in the mess-cart drawn up to receive the loot!

The men did not let the opportunity slip by without giving vent to a lot of criticism.

The subaltern's ears tingled at the remarks that he heard. Never in his life had he felt so ridiculous.

Luckily, another similar incident relieved the situation, shortly afterwards. During a few minutes' halt, a cow near the road stood gazing, with that apathetic interest peculiar to cows, at the thirsty men. It was not for nothing, as the French say, that one of the reservists had been a farm hand. He went up to the cow, unfastening his empty water-bottle as he went, and calmly leant down and began to milk the neglected animal until his bottle was full. It was not in itself a funny proceeding, but there was something about the calmness of both the cow and the man, and something about the queerness of the occasion, that appealed to the sense of humour of the dourest old puritan of them all. They laughed, they roared, they shouted, in a way that reminded the subaltern of the last "soccer" season.

The noise must have mystified the pursuing Uhlans not a little.

But the laugh did not last long on their lips. Directly afterwards they swung into a road already occupied by a train of refugees. After the sight of a good strong man struck down in his strength, this, perhaps, was the saddest sight of the whole war. How miserable they were, these helpless, hopeless people, trailing sadly along the road, the majority with all they had saved from the wreckage of their homes tied in a sheet, and carried on their backs. Some were leading a cow, others riding a horse, a few were in oxen-driven wagons. They looked as if they had lost faith in everything, even in God. They had the air of people calmly trying to realise the magnitude of the calamity which had befallen them, and failing.

Here and there the subaltern thought he saw a gleam of reproach in their faces. It hurt him not a little. Only a few days ago the British had been advancing, as they thought, to certain victory. All had been sunshine, or at any rate hope. How the villagers had shouted and cheered them! How the women had wept with sheer joy, and shy young girls had thrust flowers into their buttonholes! What heroes they had felt swinging forward to meet the enemy, to defend the homes of their friends and Allies, and avenge their wrongs!

The *rôle* had been melodramatic, superb! But here they were, skirting the very gates of Paris, apparently fleeing before the enemy, and this without having made any very determined effort at resistance. Poor protectors they must have looked! Those simple peasants would not understand the efficacy, the necessity even, of running away "to live and fight another day," with a greater chance of success.

The subaltern often used to wonder what the poor wretches thought of troops, which, though in possession of arms and ammunition, still retreated—always retreated. They could not understand.

The march came to an end about one o'clock. A halt of half-an-hour for dinner was ordered in the shade of some huge trees in a park. The mess-cart and cookers arrived, and a meal was soon in progress. The regimental officer of what is now referred to as the "Old Army" was perhaps the best-mannered man one could possibly meet. His training in the mess made him so. He was the sort of man who would not have done anything which so much as even suggested rudeness or greed. He was as scrupulous of his mess rules as a Roman Catholic priest is of his conduct at High Mass. To the newly-joined subaltern, Guest Night conveyed the holy impression of a religious rite. But here was a comic demonstration of the fact that the strictest training is only, after all, a veneer. Two senior officers were actually squabbling about a quarter-pound tin of marmalade! The subaltern could not help smiling. The incident merely showed how raw and jagged the Great Retreat had left the nerves of those who survived it.

An hour's halt passed only too soon, and its later moments were made uneasy by the instinctive aversion which everyone felt for the sound of the whistles that would mark the end of it. The battalion, however, had no sooner swung into the road, than the colonel, who had been reading a message with an expression of surprise, held up his hand to signal the halt. The moment was historic. Although none knew, it was the end of the Great Retreat.

CHAPTER 16

The Turn of the Tide

The next day the battalion linked up with the brigade, and instead of proceeding in the usual direction—southwards—they turned to the north.

There was a great deal of subdued excitement. They were not going to move off for a precious hour or so, and, as "battle seemed imminent," the subaltern did his best to make up the "deficiencies" in his equipment.

Another subaltern lay stricken with dysentery in one of the regimental wagons, and he "borrowed" his revolver and ammunition. Apart from the fact that the poor fellow was in too great pain to dispute the robbery, he declared with embellishments that he never wanted to see the —— thing again. "Take it, and be —— to it!" he said.

Curiously enough, the subaltern was able to stick to the loan through all the troubles that followed, and was eventually able to return it to its owner, met casually in the London Hippodrome, months later.

Soon afterwards, when they were marching through a village called Chaumes, he learnt that in the forthcoming battle they were to be in general reserve, and this relieved the nervous tension for the moment. There was a feeling that a great chance of distinguished service was lost, but as the general reserves are usually flung into the fight towards its concluding stages, he did not worry on that score.

The four regiments of the brigade were massed in very close formation in a large orchard, ready to move at a moment's notice. There they lay all day, sleeping with their rifles in their hands, or lying flat on their backs gazing at the intense blue of the sky overhead.

The heat, although they were in the first week in September, was greater than ever. The blue atmosphere seemed to quiver with the shock of guns.

General Headquarters had been established in a house nearby, a middle-class, flamboyant, jerry-built affair. How its owner would have gasped if he could have seen the field-marshal conducting the British share of the great battle in his immodest "*salle à manger!*"

Aeroplanes were continually ascending from and descending to a ploughed field adjacent to the orchard. Motors were ceaselessly dashing up and down. Assuredly they were near to the heart of things.

That afternoon someone procured a page of the *Daily Mirror*, which printed the first casualty list of the war. Perhaps you can remember reading it. One was not used to the sensation. One felt that "it brought things home to one." Not that this was by any means necessary at that time and place. Still it was very depressing to think that in God's beautiful sunlight, brave, strong men were being maimed and laid low for ever. One had a vague feeling that it was blasphemous, and ought to be stopped.

It was not until dusk that a start was made, and the regiment halted again about a mile further on and settled down for the night in a stubble field opposite a very imposing *château*.

Evidently the fight had gone well, for they passed at least two lines of hasty trenches quite deserted.

The Germans had at last been driven back!

Any joy that this discovery might have occasioned was sobered and tempered by the sight of small bodies of men bent double over their work in the purple twilight. They were burying-parties. Two twigs tied together and stuck in the brown mounds of earth was all the evidence there was of each little tragedy. During the retreat the subaltern had naturally had little opportunity to realise this most pitiable side of war, the cold *Aftermath of Battle*.

I will tell you of the inglorious way in which one man spent this momentous day, the wonderful hours in which the tide turned, and a continent was saved—in chasing chickens! He was the mess sergeant, and it was his duty. Anyway, the mess dined gloriously off the chickens he caught, and as a couple of hayricks had been dismantled and distributed, everybody spent a tolerably comfortable night.

Chapter 17

The Advance Begins

Although they stood to arms at the first flush of daylight on the following day, they did not march off until nearly eleven o'clock. The men were moved into the leafy grounds of the *château* to keep them out of the sun, and beyond the observation of hostile aircraft.

The regimental butchers slew one or two sheep during the wait; but the meat subsequently proved to be abominably tough, and the fat collected to oil the bolts of the men's rifles only served to make them stiffer than ever.

The subaltern had entertained fond hopes that owing to his recent unusually long hours of sleep he would not be attacked by the same nauseating sensations of fatigue; but his hopes were vain. The sleep seemed to have made things worse. A little rest had developed an over-whelming desire for more, and he felt worse than ever.

He longed as he had never longed before for long cool drinks and clean white sheets. He imagined himself at home. What would he do? He pictured himself in the bathroom eagerly peeling off his puttees as the water splashed into the pale blue bath. How he would wallow in it! He could feel how the water would caress his body, tepid and soothing.

On the table in the dining-room, green and cool with its view of the sombre pine wood, stood a long cold drink of what? Cider, per-haps, or lime-juice and soda, something you could drink and drink and drink. Last of all—culminating pleasure of heaven—his red bed-room, with the sheets ready turned down for him, soft and white and alluring. That would have been heaven.

But this heaven of his was very far away from the hard dusty road and the eternal poplars! With a painful jolt his thoughts would return to the realities of life; he would feel dazed and annoyed, and in his heart of hearts he wanted to cry.

★★★★★★

Sir Archibald Murray passed in a car, holding an animated conversation with a much-beribboned and distinguished-looking French general. He looked very pleased with himself, as well he might, for the greatest work of his career had begun the day before with astounding success.

The subaltern must have felt very tired and dissatisfied that afternoon. Having exhausted the painful thoughts of home, he began to tell himself what an awful life active service was. It never occurred to him to be thankful that a youth so young should have the luck to play his part in such tremendous events. He did not at the time realise that there were thousands of adventurous souls at home who would have given an arm to have been where he had been.

He did not realise that in after days the memory of every weary hour of trudging, of every bullet that had hummed by, and of every shell that had burst, would be a joy forever. The thought had never struck any of them, unsentimental souls!

At this point his memory confessedly breaks down. He remembers perfectly a certain "ten minutes' halt" spent in the shade of a sheaf of corn. He remembers plunging into a pine forest; but thenceforward there is a blank. His memory snaps. He cannot recollect passing through that wood, much less passing out of it. A link in the chain of his memory must have snapped.

When next he recollects anything clearly it may have been that night, the next night, or the night after that. Anyway, it was very dark, and the battalion was eventually halted in an open field. Somehow or other, straw was procured for the rest, but his own platoon was sent forward to hold an outpost position along the banks of a small stream.

Although in the daytime the sun shone with undiminished fervour, the nights were getting certainly far more chilly than they had been in August. But when one has to get up at daybreak, having never had more than four hours sleep, one does not notice it much.

During the night a fresh draft arrived.

The next morning they very soon encountered an entirely new sight, a French village hastily evacuated by the enemy. At least half of the houses had been broken into, and all the shops and inns. The Germans had dragged chairs and tables to the roadside, and they must have been sitting there drinking and smoking when the news of the

British advance, and orders to retire had come upon them. Everything seemed to show that the enemy had left at the shortest notice. He had not had time to perpetrate any of his well-known barbarities on the few inhabitants who had remained in their houses, and no attempt had apparently been made even to burn the village!

A little further on, the abstemious Hun had obviously made a halt. The litter of bottles was appalling. There was a perfect wall of them for about a quarter of a mile. The proportion of bottles to the number of men estimated to occupy four hundred yards (1000) was alarming. There must have been enough drink to upset a British Army corps. Most certainly the Germans in front must have been out of hand, and very drunk. The men were vastly amused.

The day dragged on very wearily, and no deployment was made. Apparently the enemy had taken about as much as he could comfortably endure on the previous two days. He was not waiting to be pushed back; he was speeding north-east as fast as his legs could carry him.

In the afternoon a heavy shower rather damped the excitement evoked by the enemy's dramatic failure to hold his own. Sounds of a fierce encounter were heard in front, and the brigade was hurried down a steep and wooded decline to the scene of action. They arrived too late to share in the actual infliction of defeat upon the enemy, but they were immediately sent in pursuit, as the other brigade was very tired and rather shaken.

A man told the subaltern that some unfortunate company, marching in fours up a village street, had been fired upon by a machine-gun controlled by a few men left behind by the enemy to inflict the greatest possible damage before discovery and capture. They had done their work well, for, concealed in the roof of a house, they had swept the street at point-blank range and literally mown down a whole company before they had been located, and "put out of action." Still they must have been brave men, for the personal result of such an exploit is certain death.

The state of that street had better not be described. The *Aftermath of Battle!* It is depressing, cold and passionless, dirty and bloody; the electricity of life has gone from the air, and the wine of life-blood is spilt, it seems, so needlessly upon the ground. Perhaps the spirits of the dead linger over it. Their presence is instinctively felt. As, overpowered with the sorrow of it, you pass by, the thought steals into your mind, "When will my turn come?" This *Aftermath of Battle* is assuredly the most awful thing in war.

As soon as the men began to scale the steep incline opposite, they saw that the costs had not been paid by the British alone. Figures, covered in most cases by their own grey overcoats, lay out upon the ground. Leaning up against a wall a body was still lolling. It was a sight that no one who saw it will ever forget. There was no head; it had been shorn off as cleanly as if the man had been guillotined. An unburst shell had probably swept the man's head from his shoulders as he looked over the wall, and the aimless-looking trunk was still leaning against the wall as if "waiting for further orders."

The pursuit was continued until it was quite dark. The companies wheeled into the fields, and slept where they stood. The colonel delivered a short address, which showed that all was not as well as it looked. But what really *did* worry them was lack of straw. The colonel was of the opinion that the enemy would take his stand on the opposite bank of the Marne, which, he told them, was only half a mile ahead. Tomorrow there would be a fight, the like of which neither they nor anyone else had seen before.

They were disturbed that night, not indeed by the fear of what tomorrow might hold in store, but by a small stampede of escaped horses, who careered madly over the sleeping lines, injuring one man very severely.

CHAPTER 18

The Crossing of the Marne

As soon as dawn broke—a dawn exceptionally cold and cheer-less—the cavalry pushed forward to effect some sort of reconnaissance. Meanwhile the infantry had nothing better to do than to conceal themselves behind the copses that covered the slope, and await their turn. In about an hour's time they were deployed and moved cautiously forward to the attack, the batteries being already placed in readiness for the beginning of the "show."

No army in the world can execute this movement as scientifically or as safely as the British Army. Memories of South Africa and Indian frontier fights have left us undoubtedly the finest scouting army in Europe. We were, of course, hopelessly outmatched in artillery and numbers. But artillery being equal, there was not a brigade in any army in the world that could have held its own against a British brigade. That, however, is by the way.

They pressed steadily forward, and, having breasted the slope, the valley of the Marne burst suddenly upon their view. It was at least three miles in breadth, and the opposite heights were screened by woods. A small town marked the bridge. The country was "open"—painfully open; there was not an atom of real cover between them and the heights opposite.

But no shells came whistling towards them. No doubt the enemy was holding his fire until they were within closer range. (Not a pleasant thought, this, by any means.) But no, they went on scrambling down the deep slope, and still no sound of firing disturbed the morning silence. As each moment fled by the subaltern thought to himself, "Not yet! Well, the next minute will bring things about our heads!" But the next minute kept on passing as uneventfully as its predecessors.

At last they reached the bridge and found it absolutely undamaged. Even then the subaltern could not repress the thought that all this was only a trick, and that they were being lured on to destruction. But his sanguinary forebodings were not justified, and the opposite heights were scaled without opposition.

He afterwards learnt, that, however much the Germans might have wanted to hold this magnificent line, the strategical situation had become so pressing that on this sector nothing could save them from disaster except a complete and hurried retreat. They were all but out-flanked on their right, which was already very seriously bent back; while in the centre General Foch had driven in a wedge which bade fair to crumple up the whole line.

There was nothing in any way remarkable about the little town on the other side of the river. It had the air of a neglected gutter-child, dirty and disconsolate. There were the usual signs of German occupation—broken windows, ravaged shops, and, of course, the inevitable bottles.

Here it was that the subaltern noticed for the first time that the Huns had a distinctive smell of their own. It was a curious smell, completely baffling description. If it is true that certain odours suggest certain colours, one would have described this as a brown smell, preferably a reddish-brown smell. Certain it was that the enemy left it behind him wherever he had been, as sure a clue to his passing as broken wine-bottles!

The subaltern always associates the climbing of the opposite slope with pangs of a thirst so intense that he almost forgot to wonder why the Germans had evacuated so excellent a position without firing a single shot. But headquarters were evidently not going to allow them to push forward into some previously arranged trap. Having by three o'clock in the afternoon firmly established themselves on the wooded crests of the slope, they were "pulled up" while a further reconnaissance was being made. Meanwhile, a sort of outpost position was taken up.

The subaltern's platoon was to guard the back edge of a wood, and as he established his supports in a farm, most of his men were able to fill their water-bottles, have a wash and brush up, and generally prepare themselves for whatever the next move might be. The farmer and his wife, who had remained in their home, did everything that was required of them; but he could not help noticing that the old couple did not seem as pleased at their Allies' success as one would have naturally expected. The reason was soon forthcoming. Following his usual plan of getting as much information as possible out of the French, he heard the old man, who seemed unaccountably shy and diffident, mutter casually—

"*J'ai pensé que vous ètiez tous partis hier soir.*"

"*Comment?*" said he, "*tous partis? Mais, Monsieur, nous sommes les premiers Anglais qui sont arrivés ici.*"

"*Mais, Monsieur! Anglais? Ce n'est pas possible!*"

"*C'est vrai, assurément.*"

"*Mais, L'Armée Anglaise porte toujours les habits rouges!*"

The subaltern laughed outright. This simple fellow actually believed that the English fought in scarlet. Even now he was not thoroughly convinced that they really were English. Ignorance goes hand in hand with obstinacy, and these simple old peasant folk defended their stupidity with a veritable wall of impenetrable incredulity.

The subaltern was still laboriously engaged in explaining matters to the man, when part of the headquarter's staff trotted up the road with a clatter and a swing and scurry that looked as if they were wanted very urgently on the left. It was the first time during the campaign that he had seen the corps commander and the chief of the general staff on horseback.

It must have been about five o'clock when he received a message to concentrate on the main road. On the way he was accosted by a woman perfectly distraught with grief, who explained that two days ago her little son had disappeared into "*ce bois là*" never to come out again.

"*Si votre fils vive encore, il reviendra, bien sûr, Madame. S'il est mort, moi, je ne peux pas vous aider.*" Terrible to relate, the sight of such grief annoyed rather than saddened him.

The advance was continued until it was quite dark, when the battalion denuded the usual hayrick, and "dossed down" in the usual stubble field.

CHAPTER 19

An Advanced-Guard Action

At about eleven o'clock the next morning his company commander—the captain was leading as the major was now second in command of the battalion—told the subaltern to ride back to the transport wagons and get some fresh maps and some chocolate which he had left in one of the carts. It was pleasant to get a ride, and to rest one's feet for awhile, so he took his time in getting back to the transport.

No sooner had he reached the wagons than a gun boomed. He thought nothing of that, however. Guns were always going off, at the oddest times, and without any apparent reason. Four seconds later another rolled out, followed closely by a third, fourth and fifth. Soon a regular cannonade broke out. There was obviously mischief in the air, so he crammed the maps hastily into his haversack and the chocolate into his pocket and regained the battalion as soon as he could on the exhausted animal. Even as he was pressing forward, he heard the crackle of musketry somewhere out of sight on the left.

Of course, the very thing that he had feared had happened. His company had been rapidly deployed and had already disappeared over the crest. He explained matters to the major who was in command of the remainder during the colonel's absence; dismounted, and set off on foot towards the sounds of the firing. He ran against the company sergeant-major in charge of the ammunition, who told him where his platoon was.

The next thing was to cross the fire-swept crest. Now, crossing fire-swept crests is manifestly unpleasant—especially if you are alone. If you are leading fifty men at least one and half times as old as you are, who look to you for guidance and control, it is not so bad. Bravery is very closely allied to "conspicuous gallantry," and "conspicuous gallantry" in the field is almost impossible when there is no one to look on. But he was too tired to worry much whether he was hit or not, and his platoon had to be reached as soon as possible.

He found them lined up behind a small bank, waiting for orders to reinforce the first line. Taking his glasses out of their case, he crawled forward to have a look at the position for himself. The platoon in front was established behind a mud bank, firing occasional shots at the enemy, who appeared to have dug himself in behind a railway cutting at least five hundred yards distant. Although bullets were humming pretty thickly through the air, the casualties on the British side so far were only two or three men slightly wounded. They had orders to "hang on" to that position until the centre and right should be sufficiently strengthened for the main attack to materialise, when they were to push on as best they might. Having learnt this, the subaltern crawled back, and sent out three men "to establish touch" with the front platoon.

An hour passed before anything further happened. During that time the platoon sergeant told him of the great difficulty they had had in reaching this advanced position at all, as they had been shelled from the front by the enemy, and from the left by their own batteries. Accidents such as this often happened, and the artillery were not really as culpable as would at first sight appear. Advanced-guard actions materialised so suddenly, and situations changed so quickly, that it was not always possible to circulate precise orders. The gunners' ideas of the relative positions seemed to be, during the opening stages of the attack, rather hazy—a fact that was very much resented by the men. "We ain't come out 'ere to be targets to them ruddy gunners," one fellow grumbled.

Soon, however, things straightened out, and in an hour's time the various movements preparatory to the attack had been completed. The enemy, seeing that he was almost surrounded, and that it would be impossible to extricate the greater part of his command from the battle, resolved at least to save his guns, which were accordingly withdrawn.

When at length the subaltern's platoon pushed forward in the wake of the leading platoon, no less a personage appeared unaccountably on the scene than the colonel. He had thrown off the worried look that had been growing on him of late. Some of the officers, too junior to understand how uneasy lies the head that is crowned with the responsibility for many lives, had been heard to say that the colonel's manner and general outlook upon the campaign was tinged with unnecessary anxiety, and that he had no right to allow the Germans to disturb his peace of mind. If this were so, the presence of actual and tangible danger completely obliterated all traces of nerves. He stood up in the firing-line. He drew himself up to the full of his height, and seemed to inhale with pleasure the dangerous air. All the time bullets were humming overhead like swift and malignant insects, or striking the ground with a spatter of brown earth.

The adjutant, following him, suddenly bent double as if he had been struck below the belt; but the colonel merely straightened himself, and not a nerve in his phlegmatic face twitched.

"What's the matter?" asked the colonel.

"Only a bullet struck my revolver hilt, sir," replied the adjutant. It had splintered the woodwork and been deflected between his arm and ribs.

Near by a man rose on his knees to get a better shot at the enemy.

"What's that man doing? Get down there this moment!" roared the colonel.

Then, as he recognised an old soldier of the regiment, "Atkins, how dare you expose yourself unnecessarily? Your wife used to do my washing in Tidshot. Me? Oh, I'm only an old bachelor. It doesn't matter about me. There's nobody to care what happens to me." And, well pleased with his joke, the colonel passed down the line, proud of his magnificent bravery.

There is something about the rough-and-tumble of battle that lifts one above one's self. One's legs and arms are not the same listless limbs that were crying for rest only a short hour ago. One is envigoured; the excitement stimulates. One feels great, magnanimous, superb. The difficulty lies not in forcing oneself to be brave, but in curbing ridiculous impulses, and in forcing the brain to work slowly and smoothly. The smallest natures rise to great heights. An ordinary self-centred creature performs acts of dazzling generosity towards fellows he does not even know—with everything to lose and nothing to gain. He will rescue a wounded man under heavy fire, to whom an hour previously he would have refused to lend sixpence.

Why is it?

If the enemy were a roaring brazen beast, such as the knights of the fairy tales used to fight, one could understand it. But he is not. You cannot even see him. Three-quarters of a mile ahead there is a dark brown line, and that is all. Whence comes the love of battle? Is it roused by the little messengers of death that whizz invisibly by? No one can say; the whole feeling is most probably the result of imagination and desire to do great things.

On they swept. The leading platoon was now covering the ground at such a pace that it was impossible to catch up with them. As the ground was open the whole line could be seen sweeping forward to engulf the enemy. The long dotted lines of brown advanced steadily and inexorably. Line upon line of them breasted the crest, and followed in the wake of the leading wave. It was scarcely a spectacular sight, yet it was the vindication of the British methods of attack.

The wild firing of the Germans had little effect. Curiously enough, the line that suffered least was the first, and even in the others the casualties were negligible. And all the time they were nearing the railway bank.

But the end was in sight, and the enemy realised that further resistance would be useless. They were caught. About half a dozen men sprang on to the railway bank and began furiously to wag white sheets of paper or rag—anything white. They must have been brave men to do such a thing. The British gunners either did not see their signs, or perhaps refused to accept them on account of various "jokes" that the enemy had at other times played with the white flag. Anyway the firing continued with unabated fury. They stood there to the end without flinching, and when they fell other men took their places. It is mean and untruthful to say that the Germans are cowards. Certain it was that their pathetic bravery—there is always something sad about bravery—so touched the British that they accepted the surrender without reserve or suspicion. Even the artillery ceased fire.

At this point the leading platoon broke clean away. They could not be held in. The orderly advance degenerated into a wild dash. Men bent double and rushed. Determination was written on each flushed face. The Germans must have been terrified; it looked as if they were to be bayoneted as they stood, with their arms raised in surrender. It must have been a very trying moment for them, indeed, as the British raced towards them up the incline. The leading men were soon clambering up the embankment. What would happen? Was a disgraceful and bloody massacre about to begin? The excitement was intense. The subaltern ran on harder than ever, with some vague idea of "stopping a scene," but he need not have bothered. The men were not out for blood or scalps. All they wanted was souvenirs or helmets!

They got them with such success that there was little left for the other platoons.

When the subaltern came up the "show" was over. There were a great many dead Germans lying, as they had died, behind the embankment. The thought of taking something which they had worn never occurred to him. If it had been he would have dismissed it on the grounds that there was no means of sending such things home, while to add to the weight and worry of his kit by carrying a "*Pickelhaube*" about, indefinitely, for the rest of the campaign, was, of course, unthinkable.

Then the "rally" sounded, and the companies that had taken part in the attack began to re-form. There was a considerable delay before two of the platoons appeared at the rallying point. The men did not come in a body but by driblets. He began to get nervous about the other two subalterns, and in a few minutes went to see what had happened to them.

"Lord bless you, sir, 'e's all right," said a man in answer to the subaltern's inquiry. "We wouldn't let no harm come to '*im*." The man who spoke was an old soldier whom he knew well, tall, wiry, commanding—the sort of man that a young officer leans upon, and who, reciprocally, relies on his officer. In the old peace days, if any special job that required intelligence or reliance were going, he always saw that this man got it. He had made a sort of pet of him; and now he was openly, frankly displaying a state of mind akin to worship towards another officer. It was defection, rank desertion. A ridiculous feeling of jealousy surged up in the subaltern's mind, as he turned back towards the company.

As he regained the road, many stretchers passed. They were no longer things of tragedy, to be passed by with a shudder and averted eyes—he was getting used to horror.

CHAPTER 20

Defence

It was now midday, and the officers of the two companies that had been deployed gathered round the mess-cart. The remaining companies, who had been kept in local reserve during the fight, were sent out to bury the dead. The rain began to fall in torrents, and somehow the memory of crouching under the mess-cart to get shelter has left a far more definite and indelible impression upon the subaltern's mind than the actual moments of danger and excitement.

A large band of prisoners had been captured by our troops that day. Small detachments had from time to time been captured ever since the turn at Chaumes, but this was different. There were long lines of them, standing bolt upright, and weaponless. The subaltern looked at them curiously. They struck him as on the whole taller than the English, and their faces were not brown, but grey. He admired their coats, there was a martial air in the long sweep of them. And he confessed that one looked far more of a soldier in a helmet. There is a ferocity about the things, a grimness well suited to a soldier. . . . Not that clothes make the man.

He sternly refused himself the pleasure of going to get a closer sight of them. He wanted very badly to see them, perhaps to talk French with them, but a feeling that it was perhaps *infra dignitatem* debarred him. The men, however, had no such scruples. They crowded round their captives, and slowly and silently surveyed them. They looked at them with the same sort of interest that one displays towards an animal in the zoo, and the Germans paid just as much attention to their regard as zoo animals do. Considering that only a short hour ago they had been trying to take each other's lives, there seemed to be an appalling lack of emotion in either party. Fully half an hour the Tommies inspected them thus. Then, with infinite deliberation, one man produced a packet of "*Caporal*" cigarettes and offered one, with an impassive countenance, to a German. As far as the subaltern could see, not a single word was exchanged nor a gesture made. They did not move away until it was time to fall in.

The advance was continued until it was dark, and intermittent firing was heard throughout the afternoon on either flank. The German retreat, which had in its first stages been conducted with such masterly skill, was rapidly developing into a hurried and ill-conducted movement, that bade fair to lead to disaster. Reports of large quantities of prisoners were coming in more frequently than ever.

It was at this time that the subaltern first heard the now notorious story of the German who had been at the Savoy, and who gave himself up to the officer whom he recognised as an old *habitué*. One of the officers in the regiment said that this had happened to him, and was believed—for the moment. Later on, officers out of every corps solemnly related similar experiences, with occasional variations in the name of the hotel. Usually it was the Savoy or the Ritz; less often the Carlton, or even the Cecil, but the "Pic" or the "Troc" were absolutely barred. The story multiplied so exceedingly that one began to suspect that the entire German corps in front was exclusively composed of ex-waiters of smart London hotels.

Another sign that the Germans were beginning to be thrust back more quickly than they liked was the frequent abandonment of transport. Whole trains of motor lorries that had been hastily burned and left by the roadside, and all sorts of vehicles with broken wheels, were constantly being passed. The subaltern remembers seeing a governess cart, and wondering what use the Germans had found for it. Perhaps a German colonel had been driven gravely in it, at the head of his men. He wondered whether the solemn Huns would have been capable of seeing the humour of such a situation.

Horses, too, seemed to have been slaughtered by the score. They looked like toy horses, nursery things of wood. Their faces were so unreal, their expressions so glassy. They lay in such odd postures, with their hoofs sticking so stiffly in the air. It seemed as if they were toys, and were lying just as children had upset them. Even their dimensions seemed absurd. Their bodies had swollen to tremendous sizes, destroying the symmetry of life, confirming the illusion of unreality.

The sight of these carcases burning in the sun, with buzzing myriads of flies scintillating duskily over their unshod hides, excited a pity that was almost as deep as his pity for slain human beings. After all, men came to the war with few illusions, and a very complete knowledge of the price to be paid. They knew why they were there, what they were doing, and what they might expect. They could be buoyed up by victory, downcast by defeat. Above all, they had a *cause*, something to fight for, and if *fate* should so decree, something to die for. But these horses were different; they could neither know nor understand these things. Poor, dumb animals, a few weeks ago they had been drawing their carts, eating their oats, and grazing contentedly in their fields. And then suddenly they were seized by masters they did not know, raced away to places foreign to them, made to draw loads too great for them, tended irregularly, or not at all, and when their strength failed, and they could no longer do their work, a bullet through the brain ended their misery. Their lot was almost worse than the soldiers'!

To the subaltern it seemed an added indictment of war that these wretched animals should be flung into that vortex of slaughter. He pitied them intensely, the sight of them hurt him; and the smell of them nauseated him. Every memory of the whole advance is saturated with that odour. It was pungent, vigorous, demoralising. It filled the air, and one's lungs shrank before it. Once, when a man drove his pick through the crisp, inflated side, a gas spurted out that was positively asphyxiating and intolerable.

However much transport the Germans abandoned, however severe the losses they sustained, they always found time to break open every *estaminet* they passed, and drain it dry. Wretched inns and broken bottles proved to be just as reliable a clue to their passing as the smell of them.

Chapter 21

The Defence of the Brandy

The next morning two companies were detached from the battalion as escort to a brigade of artillery. The other two companies, who had returned during the night, did not seem to be greatly upset by their gruesome task of burying the dead.

They did not come in contact with the enemy, and no outstanding incident impressed itself upon the subaltern's mind. The heat had abated with dramatic swiftness. A wind that was almost chilly swept the plains, driving grey clouds continually across the sun. The summer was over. That day they joined battle with the outposts of a foe that was to prove more hateful and persistent than the German winter.

The name of a village known as Suchy-le-Château figured on many of the signposts that they passed, but they never arrived there, and, branching off east of Braisne, they came upon the remainder of the Battalion, drawn up in a stubble field.

A driving rain had begun to fall early in the afternoon, and when at length the march was finished their condition was deplorable. Though tired out with a long day's march, they dared not rest, because to lie down in the sodden straw was to court sickness. Their boots, worn and unsoled, offered no resistance whatever to the damp. Very soon they could hear their sodden socks squelching with water as they walked. A night of veritable horror lay in front of them; they were appalled with the prospect of it. The rain seemed to mock at the completeness of their misery.

However, the *fates* were kind, for the general, happening to pass, took pity on them and allowed them to be billeted in the outhouses of a farm nearby. The sense of relief which this move gave to the subaltern was too huge to describe. Contentment took possession of him utterly. The tension of his nerves and muscles relaxed: he thought that the worries and hardships of that day, at least, were over.

But he was wrong.

No sooner had his platoon wearily thrown their rifles and equipment into the musty barn that was allotted to them, than the colonel told him that he would have to sleep with his men, the reason being that the owner of the farm, on the approach of the Germans, had hidden a large stock of brandy beneath the straw in the very barn that his men had entered. The farmer had asked the colonel to save his liquor from the troops, and the colonel, with horrible visions of a regiment unmanageable and madly intoxicated before his eyes, replied that most assuredly he would see that the men did not get hold of the brandy. The subaltern told his sergeant, but otherwise the proximity of bliss was kept a strict secret from the men.

Throughout the whole of that long day the subaltern had been looking forward to, longing for, and idealising the rest which was to follow after the labours of the day. And now that it had at last been achieved, it proved to be a very poor imitation of the ideal rest and slumber that he had been yearning for. To begin with, the delays before quarters were settled upon were interminable. And then this news about the brandy. The evening meal was delayed almost a couple of hours, and every minute of the delay annoyed him, because it was so much precious time for sleep lost. Even when the meal arrived, it proved to be insufficient, and he was still hungry, cold and damp, when at last he hobbled across the yard to the barn.

The place had no ventilation. The air was foul with the smell of damp grain, and men, and wet boots. He hesitated at the door; he would rather have slept in the open air, but the yard was inches deep in mud and manure. He groped forward, and at every inch that he penetrated further into the place, the air seemed to become thicker, more humid, more foul. In the thick darkness his foot stumbled on the sleeping form of a man, who rolled over and swore drowsily. At last, after interminable feeling in the darkness, and balancing himself on sacks of grain, he attained the corner where the bottles lay buried, and threw himself down to sleep.

But sleep was impossible. In spite of the insupportable atmosphere he remained cold. Every second someone was moving! One instant a man would shuffle and cough in one corner, then someone would grunt and groan as he turned restlessly in his sleep, and the happier few who had achieved slumber would snore laboriously. Now and then a man would rise shakily to his feet and thread his way unsteadily to the door, kicking up against recumbent forms as he went, and evoking language as murky as the atmosphere. The subaltern felt a savage joy in the recriminations and expletives that filled the air. Like lightning, they relieved the thunder-pressure of the air.

CHAPTER 22

Strategy As You Like It

Dawn found them already paraded in the farmyard, shivering, and not much better rested than when they had entered the barn of dreadful memory the night before. Each day the accumulation of fatigue and nerve-strain became greater; each day it grew harder to drag the weary body to its feet, and trudge onwards. Though the tide of victory had turned, though every yard they covered was precious ground re-won, they longed very intensely for a lull. The subaltern felt in a dim way that the point beyond which flesh and blood could not endure was not very far ahead. As it was, he marvelled at himself.

During the course of the morning the captain returned to the company, with a little map, and a great deal of information concerning the strategy of the war, about which everybody knew so little.

To begin at the beginning, he said that the Allies had begun the campaign under two great disadvantages. The first was their very serious numerical inferiority in forces that could be immediately used. If numbers alone counted, the Germans were bound to win until the French were fully mobilised.

The other disadvantage was the preconceived notion that the German Government would keep its word with regard to the violation of Belgian neutrality. If this had been observed, it would have been almost a strategical impossibility to turn the Allied left flank. The attack in force was expected to be made in the Lorraine area. Consequently, when it became evident that the main German effort was to be launched through Belgium, all preconceived plans of French concentration had either to be abandoned, or, at any rate, greatly modified in order to meet the enemy offensive from an unexpected quarter.

After their unexpected setback at Liège, the invaders met with little resistance from the Belgian army, which was, of course, hopelessly outnumbered, and their armies were rapidly forming up on a line north of the Sambre, which roughly extended south-east by east to north-west by west. Meanwhile, the initial French offensive which had been launched in the region of the Vosges had resulted in the temporary capture of Mülhouse, and had then been abandoned in order to face the threatening disaster from the north.

It was thought advisable to wait until the concentration of the English Army was completed, then, to comply with an obvious rule of strategy which says, *"Always close with your enemy when and wherever he shows himself, in order to discover and hold him to his dispositions,"* a general advance was made along the whole centre and left of the Allied line. The line swung forward, and perhaps someday one of the handful of men who know will tell exactly what was the object of this move-ment. Was it meant to join battle in all seriousness with the enemy, and to drive him from Belgium, or was it just a precautionary measure to hold and delay him? Probably the latter. The Allied *generalissimo* had probably made up his mind to the fact that the first battle—the battle in Belgium—was already lost by the Allies' lateness in concentration. Regarded in this light the battle in Belgium was undoubtedly the greatest rear-guard action in history.

On account of a possible underestimation of the enemy's strength, and of the completeness of his dispositions, the Allies found them-selves, when the lines first clashed, in a more serious position than they probably anticipated. The enemy gained two initial successes that decided, past doubt, the fate of the battle which was now raging along the whole front from Mons to Mülhouse. Namur, the fortress which had enjoyed a reputation as the Port Arthur of Europe, fell before the weight of the German siege howitzer in a few days. The magnitude of the disaster appalled the whole world, for indirectly the piercing of these forts laid open the road to Paris.

Nor was this all. The enemy forced the passage of the Sambre at Charleroi, and threatened to cut the Allied centre from the left. The British Army, on the extreme left, found itself confronted by a numer-ical superiority of nearly three to one, while its left flank and lines of communication with Havre were seriously menaced by a huge body of Uhlan cavalry. In a word, the positions taken up by the whole of the Allied centre and left were no longer tenable. To hang on would have been to court disaster. There was nothing for it but to cut and go.

But the Allies did not meet with the same ill luck along the whole line. The small successes gained on the right, in Alsace, had apparently been consolidated. The German tide through Luxembourg was stemmed, and, even though the *Kaiser* himself witnessed its bombardment, Nancy held out. But the trump card in the Allies' hand was Verdun. De Castlenau clung resolutely to the chain of forts crowning the heights in front of the town, and his successful defence saved Paris. Whatever might happen to the centre and left, the right, at any rate, seemed safe.

The Allied *generalissimo* was forced to give way before the fury of the German onslaught in Belgium. He withdrew his armies while there was yet time, thus averting irrevocable disaster. According to all the rules of the game, he should have retired his whole line southwards, in order to ensure the safety of Paris. But he did not throw his highest trump: he clung to Verdun, and left Paris exposed. His armies retreated, not on the capital, but in a sweeping movement that was hinged upon Verdun. He realised that the fate of Paris depended not upon its being covered by the Allies, but upon the fate of the second great battle of the war.

Meanwhile, the great retreat—this hinging movement—continued, very slowly near Verdun, very, very swiftly on the left. Days passed; no attempt was made to check the enemy's advance, and the passing of each day left Paris more exposed. The world gasped at the breathless swiftness with which disaster seemed to be swooping down upon the capital. But every day de Castlenau was consolidating his defence of Verdun, in face of tremendous odds; and every day the ferocity of the German onrush waned.

The line continued to swing resolutely back, until such time as a completed mobilisation should allow the Allies to turn upon the enemy in greater force, in their own time, and on chosen ground. A premature effort would have spoiled all. They had to wait for their chance.

Meanwhile, rapid concentrations of reserves were taking place behind the line, the most famous instance of which was the reserve army moved out of Paris by General Galliéni in taxis, *fiacres*, and any vehicle the authorities could commandeer to ensure that the army should be in its place in time. It was in its place.

Just as the world was beginning to say that the war was over, General Joffre decided that the iron was hot, that the time to strike had arrived. "The moment has come," he wrote, "to die where you stand, rather than give way."

The outlook changed from black to rose with the completeness and ease of a pantomime transformation scene. The Verdun heights remained impregnable. The whole line turned and fought where it stood. The enemy, worn out by his exertions, stretched his line of communications to breaking-point, and it was said that his supplies of food and munitions had come temporarily very near to collapse. The Allies checked him. He could not even hold his own. In two days he was moving back, away from Paris.

The economic reasons were not the only factors in his downfall. He was beaten by the Allied morale, and also by the Allied strategy. Von Kluck, the commander of the German right, hurrying on in an abortive pursuit of the British Army, found that he was outflanked by the army of Galliéni, which, stronger than his own, threatened his line of communications. To press on towards Paris would have been suicidal. To linger in his present position would have been to court capture. He, therefore, began the famous march across the French front, by which he hoped to gain touch with the army on his left, and as he turned, the British and French fell upon him simultaneously, as in a vice. For a day the line wavered irresolutely, then Von Kluck realised that the pendulum of success was beginning to swing the other way. He had to retire or face irretrievable disaster.

Thus Paris was saved. The tremendous blow aimed at it was parried, and it seemed as if the striker tottered, as if he had overreached his strength. The treachery with which the Germans had inaugurated the movement, the brutality and cruelty with which they had carried it through, were brought to nothing before the superior morale of the Allied troops, and the matchless strategy of their commander.

The enemy was checked along the whole line, but the Allies were not satisfied with that. The French flung themselves upon the invader with a ferocity and heroism that was positively reminiscent of the Napoleonic legends. General Foch, in command of the general reserve, achieved the culminating success in this victory, known as the Battle of the Marne. He broke the enemy's line: he thrust into the gap a wedge so powerful that the enemy was forced to give way on either side of it, because his centre was broken. The victory of the Marne was assured.

Slowly at first, latterly with increasing speed, the Allies were hurling the enemy northwards. He was becoming more demoralised every day. A victory even greater than the Marne was in sight.

★★★★★★

"And that," said the captain, "is where we are at present."

"They'll turn on us in a day or two, and then there'll be the devil of a fight," said the senior subaltern.

Everybody laughed at him, but they had an uneasy feeling that he would be right.

Chapter 23

The Last Advance

While he was dreaming, the time slipped by almost unnoticed. It was not until eleven o'clock that a halt was made. He could just discern in the darkness the dim outlines of what appeared to be a large farmhouse, surrounded by barns and outhouses. Some transport had got jammed in the yard. He could hear the creak of wheels, the stamping of hoofs, and shouts. There was not a light anywhere, and they waited for half-an-hour that seemed interminable, for they were drenched through, and tired, and were longing for any cover out of the wet. Sounds of shuffling were heard in front, and at last they found themselves on the move again. Another fifty yards, as far as a gate in a wall, and then they stuck again. More weary, exasperating minutes; then at last the bedraggled figure of the captain loomed out of the darkness.

"Is that you?" he asked.

"All right, lead round here!"

He led them to a large barn, and they turned in to sleep just as they were. No supper, not a fire to dry their sodden clothes, not a blanket to cover their chilled bodies.

As usual, they got to sleep somehow, and as usual dawn came about thirty hours before they were ready for it.

They moved out immediately, and continued the course of the march. The rain-laden clouds had rolled completely away. The sky looked hard and was scarcely blue; the country was swept by a strong nipping wind, for which they were very thankful, since it served to dry their clothes.

The machine-gun officer, passing down the battalion, walked with them while he told them two wonderful stories. It may have been crude, but in another way it was almost as satisfying as breakfast.

He solemnly explained to them that the war was nearly over. The Germans, lured into making this tremendous and unnecessary effort to capture Paris, had left their eastern front dangerously weak. The Russians were pouring into Germany in their millions. The Cossacks were already around Posen. Nobody quite knew where Posen was, but it sounded deliciously like Potsdam. Anyway, they would be there in a month.

A few surplus millions, who, presumably on account of the crush, could not burst into Germany by the quickest route, had been despatched, *via* Archangel, to the northern coast of Scotland. Their progress thenceforwards is, of course, notorious. By now they had safely landed at Antwerp, and had pursued a career that must have bored them as monotonously victorious. Namur, "and all those places" had been captured, and at that moment Maubeuge was being relieved. The Germans were being sandwiched between the victorious Russian, French and British arms. They could only escape as through the neck of a bottle. And the end of the war was so near, and so definite, that it almost lacked interest.

The subaltern was elated. He refused to question the likelihood of such tales. He was hungry for just such cheering stories of success. And when he got them, he devoured them with avidity, without ever looking at them. The effect on him was bracing. It was glorious, he told himself, to have taken part in such happenings. The only cloud on his horizon was the fact that the chance to do distinguished acts had never come to him. The regimental colours never required saving under heavy fire, for the simple reason that they reposed safely at the *depôt*. Neither did the colonel, a most profitable person to rescue, ever get wounded in the open, and give an opportunity for gallant rescue work. He had never had a chance to "stick a Bosch." He had never drawn his sword in a triumphant charge, never blazed his revolver in a face, never twisted a bayonet on a body. It would require courage, he told himself, to admit these things when he was back again at home.

You must not laugh at the stories of the machine-gunner. He believed what he wanted to believe. Remember, too, that the Allies were then at the zenith of the greatest victory that was achieved in the first eighteen months of the war. The strategical ideas of the machine-gunner may have been faulty, but he has saved more lives with his guns than any doctor in the land.

At about eight o'clock in the morning, the subaltern saw the company in front twisting off the road, and forming up in "mass" in the open field. They were then in the centre of a large plateau, which offered an uninterrupted view of miles of flat country on every side. A rough "outpost" disposition, with which he was fortunately not sent, was detailed, and the news was spread that there was to be a halt of several hours.

The business of drying clothes, and cleaning up, instantly began. Ingrained soldierly cleanliness of the men was displayed. Without any order, and in spite of their weariness, whenever they were halted over an hour in the daylight—which had very seldom happened—they would immediately set about shaving, and cleaning themselves and their rifles. They shaved with the cold water, poured from their water-bottles into the lids of their canteens. There was a vast rubbing of bolts, and "pulling through" of barrels. An erstwhile barber in the senior subaltern's platoon did tremendous business with a pair of scissors and a comb, his patrons being seated on an upturned ammunition-case.

They had not halted long before a "mail" came in. The subaltern was not among the lucky few who received letters or small parcels. Not that he minded much. From whomever the letter might come, or in whatever vein it had been written, he admitted to himself that he would feel savage with it, and would have dismissed it as "hot air" if it were sympathetic, or as "hard-hearted" if it were anything else.

He wrote home on the now famous postcards that inform the addressee that, on such and such a date, the sender was alive and well. He felt very relieved that at last he had an opportunity to relieve the anxiety of the people at home.

The best part of the two hours was spent in "franking"—that is censoring—his men's letters. It was a very unwelcome task, and although he thoroughly appreciated the military necessity, he cordially hated being forced, as it were, to pry into their private affairs.

Meanwhile the wind had dried them, and the sun was high in the heavens. Rations arrived, and were distributed. The sun and the tea warmed them, and in the afternoon a little sleep was possible.

The subaltern was aroused at about four o'clock, and the march was continued. The senior subaltern had received a box of Abdullas in the post, which he kindly shared with his two juniors. The cigarettes seemed enormously fat, and the tobacco extraordinarily pale. They had smoked nothing but the little "*Caporal*" French cigarettes—and not many of them—since their own supply had given out. They had said all along how much they longed for "decent English" cigarettes, and now they had got them they were not at all so sure that they liked them.

There was a lance-corporal in the company who was not as generous to his fellows as the senior subaltern had been. He smoked the cigarettes he had been sent, persistently, and with obvious enjoyment. The men around him were hungry for a "whiff"; the sight of him calmly lighting a fresh "fag" at the stump of the old maddened them beyond endurance. At length one man could bear it no longer.

"Look at 'im, a'eatin' of 'em. Lor! give a thought to yer ruddy comrades, can't yer?"

They seemed to miss tobacco more poignantly than any other luxury.

A little later, sounds of great artillery bombardments rose up in front of them and on each side, but they could not yet see any signs of a fight, as they had not yet reached the edge of the plateau.

Further on, the road descended slightly, and a very little way ahead the subaltern saw, for the first time, a battery of heavy artillery at work. The whole affair seemed to him to be singularly peaceful. The men went to work in the same efficient and rapid way that they would have done in a machine-room. Their targets were, of course, invisible, and there was no attempt to cover the guns from sight, nor to protect them from hostile shells. He was surprised to see how comparatively slowly the gun recoiled after discharge. The noise was ear-splitting, terrific.

"There'll be some fun when the transport comes along," said the senior subaltern, with unholy glee.

He was right: there probably would be a great deal of "fun." The battery was not more than fifty yards from the road on the left, while on the right there was a drop, at an angle of at least sixty degrees, of twenty yards. He imagined the frightened horses careering madly down the slope, the carts and wagons bumping and crashing down upon them—the kicking, struggling heap below!

Then, just as it was growing dark, they reached the edge of the plateau, and the huge rolling valley of the Aisne swam before them in the purple twilight. The further heights were already wrapped up in darkness; and the ground, glowing green at their feet, merged in the distance to rich velvet patches of purple and brown. The river itself was hidden by the trees clustering round its banks, but they could guess its course, winding away for a score or so of miles to the east.

"What a beautiful scene," he said reverently.

The senior subaltern may, or may not, have appreciated the beauty of the scene. His eye was on the further heights.

"This is where they will try to stand," he said.

And, as usual, he was right.

They looked across to where the dark heights opposite were thrown out clearly against the pale sky, faintly yellow with the reflected glory of the sunset at their backs. Lights momentarily twinkled, now here, now there, intermittently along the whole line, as far as they could see. It was just as if matches were being struck, and instantly blown out again. But all the time the low, booming noise floated across to them. It was the German heavy artillery, slinging over heavier projectiles than, so far, it had been their bad fortune to meet.

Just as they were entering a little village, nestling half-way down the slope, a tremendous explosion happened. There was a thunder-clap of noise, and a perfect cloud of earth and stones and wood was thrown high into the air. It was their introduction to the famous "Jack Johnson."

But, "Jack Johnson" or no "Jack Johnson," they marched on into the village, and were allotted billets for the night. The men of the company were very comfortably accommodated in a barn half filled with dry hay, which, of course, is a great deal more pleasant to sleep upon than straw. The officers went into a little cottage by the barn, and, having intimated to the owner of it that they were willing to buy anything she could sell them to eat or drink, flung off their equipment and went out into the little farmyard.

The air was rosy with the sunset light; even the rising dust was golden. The sky overhead was the palest of dusky whites. It was not a sky: it was just eternity. Out of it, infinitely far, yet comparatively close, a few stars were beginning to wink.

The men in the yard were cooking their evening meal over a few little fires, squatting over them, eyeing anxiously the brewing tea or frizzling bacon. It was impossible to feel nervous or discontented. The very atmosphere was benign. It seemed as if "God was in His Heaven," and all was well with the world.

Chapter 24

Saturday Night

Every picture wakened in the mind of the reader by the preceding chapters should be bathed in the brightest of sunshine, under the bluest of skies, and the horizons should quiver with the blue heat. From now onwards he must imagine grey skies, often streaming rain, and always muddy roads and sodden grass.

That day saw the inauguration of a new kind of misery for our troops. Dust, heat and thirst, their previous tormentors, retired in favour of mud, chill and an unappeasable hunger. Their overstrained nerves and worn bodies rendered them very susceptible even to the first breath of autumn.

The subaltern had lost all his underwear except his shirt, and part of his socks. His breeches were torn at the knee, and he felt the chill of the wind very acutely. He could feel the damp mud through the flapping toes of his boot.

Then it began to rain—no mere light summer shower, that cooled one's face and clothes, and delightfully wet one's hands, but a real autumnal downpour. Hastily he undid the straps which tied his Burberry, and shuffled into it, as he marched along. It was caked with mud, and smelt of the earth that he had so often grovelled in, but as he fastened the hooks beneath his chin, he felt profoundly glad of it, elated that he had something to keep off the chill and wet. He buttoned it down to his knees and experienced the faint sensation of comfort that one feels when drawing one's blinds to shut out a stormy night.

★★★★★★

Then the guns began to rattle by; always an ominous sign, for it meant that battle was imminent. It was a remarkable thing that neither infantry nor artillery took much notice of each other as they met. The guns and carriages would thunder and bump and clatter over the *pavé*, the thickset horses straining at their harness, the drivers urging them on. But the infantry would plod along just the same, regardless of the noise and bustle. The men would not even raise their eyes from the boots of the preceding four.

Very soon after the last gun-carriage had rattled past, sounds of a bombardment would be heard—the bangs and whizz of shells. The column would probably be halted, while a reconnaissance was made to ascertain in what force the enemy was holding his position. As a rule, deployments were not necessary, for the artillery generally succeeded in dislodging the enemy off their own bat. Such affairs as this happened no less than three times before it was dark, and in each case the Germans had had to leave their dead and wounded behind them.

One poor fellow lay with his head propped up against a heap of stones by the wayside. His chin and mouth had been torn from his face, and the ragged flesh hung in tatters, red and bleeding, as it had been torn. Almost before their eyes the man was passing away. It was awful.

"Poor devil, all this 'ere wasn't 'is fault, yer know," a man muttered.

As far as the subaltern could hear, no one answered him. Perhaps some of them were wondering where that dying man's soul was going to. One was a Christian, of course, but one wanted to know more. One wanted, very badly, a little precise, definite knowledge of *What Happens*—after. At that moment he hated *Hamlet*. Yet the words kept surging through his brain: "*To die . . . to sleep . . . in that sleep of death, what dreams may come? . . . puzzles the will . . . makes us rather bear the ills we have, than fly to others that we know not of!*"

Not that conscience had "made a coward" of him, nor of any other man or boy he had ever seen, a great deal nearer to death and vital, elementary things than Shakespeare had ever been. He felt a little foolish for it, but all the same he was thrilled by a sensation of triumphant superiority to the Bard of Avon.

All the time the rain was streaming down, and all the time their clothes grew wetter and wetter. Just before dusk a halt was made by the roadside, and at last the booming of the guns died down to a silence that was only broken by the incessant patter of the rain upon the sodden earth.

There was not much to eat, only biscuits, whose freshness and crispness had been lost in moist pockets. Nobody was thirsty: there was too much water externally!

It was quite dark when they moved on. Somehow the darkness used to come to them as a tremendous relief, as an armistice. They felt, in a subtle way, more at home in it, for it shut out from their eyes the strange sights and horrors of a land quite foreign to them. After the wearing day, it brought a freshness that was exhilarating, a refreshing coolness to the cheeks and hands that was gratifying and soothing. In spite of everything their spirits rose.

As they passed over a little railway station, innocent, as usual, of any suspicion of a platform, with a box set up as waiting-room, one of the men in the section of fours behind him stumbled heavily over the single lines.

"Nah then, Bill, wotcher doing to New Street Station?" New Street Station, with its smoke, and hurrying crowds, and shrieking steam to be compared to this clean, open, deserted spot! The daring of such a comparison was stupendous. It appealed instantly to the men's sense of the ridiculous. They roared with laughter.

The rain fell with depressing regularity, the wind blew gustily, but the ice had been broken, an example had been set, and they all vied with each other in forgetting their troubles in laughter.

"Blessed if it ain't Saturday night!" said one. It was impossible to say offhand what day it was, but after a slight argument they arrived at the astounding discovery that it was indeed Saturday. The discovery was astounding, because it was almost incredible to them that such misery could happen on a Saturday night—*the* night of the week—the night of marketing, of toothsome dishes, of melodrama and music halls.

"If my missus could see me now," roared a reservist, "wouldn't her laff!" He was, perhaps, a great deal more amused than she would have been, poor woman.

"I ain't agoing to church tomorrer," said another, with assumed languor. "I'll lay a'bed, an' smoke me baccy, an' read me Sunday papers" (derisive groans).

"Me and Sam's goin' on 'Midnight Pass' ternight, ain't we, Sam?" inquired a young "timeserving" fellow. "Who's on at the Hipperdrome?"

"Oh! Mah-rie Lloyd."

"Get urt, you'm too young to see our Mah-rie." Roars of laughter, that almost shut out the wind with their heartiness!

The subaltern could tell very accurately how their thoughts were flying homewards, and he could see the very same pictures in front of their eyes, because he lived near to where most of them lived, and knew the sights that most of them knew. Their homes on Saturday night! The warm red tiles of their kitchen floors; the "scrap" mats (laboriously hand sewn) in front of the bright fires in their "grates." The walls of their "parlours," bedecked with gorgeous lithographs, calendars and framed texts!

All the things they loved so much to do on Saturday nights. The humming market street, entirely blocked with its double rows of booths. How pleasant it must have seemed to them! At the top of the street the church stared impassively into space; at the bottom, the trams clanged and grinded as they rounded the corner and swung triumphantly into the square. The stalls, brightly lit by flaring gas-jets, laden with meat, fish, fruit, sweets, music, flowers, all that the soul could long for throughout a restful Sunday day. Their womenfolk, with their heads covered in the ubiquitous shawl of many colours, buzzing busily from booth to booth, with a purse clutched in one hand, and an open "string" bag, filled with bulky newspaper-covered parcels, in the other. The men looking on with hands in pockets, English-wise, indefinably self-conscious in the face of the delicate business of shopping. Then perhaps an hour or two's excitement in a shag-scented picture palace, or a crowded music hall with some big star at the top of the bill, a small one at the bottom, and the between turns lamentable. And, of course, a visit to some busy "saloon bar" redolent of "beer and 'baccy." Then home on the electric tram.

The thought of it all did not, as might be expected, make them sad. In fact, the home memories seemed to warm their hearts, and the humour of this "Saturday night," which might have left more delicately cultured natures untouched, appealed to them irresistibly.

That night the subaltern, too, had his dreams. They did not fly homewards: he would have hated to have been surrounded and overwhelmed by his family: he shrank at the thought of congratulations: he shuddered at the idea of explanations. Tonight he would have wished to be quite alone. And in London!

First of all would come a hot bath at the hotel—a tremendous scrubbing, and a "rub down," with a big towel—haircuttings, and shaving, and nail cleanings! Then he would get into mufti. He chose, after a careful review, a lounge suit of a grey-blue colour that had been fashionable that summer. It was light, and he had always liked the feel of it on his shoulders. He chose the shirt, collar and tie to go with it. He imagined himself completely dressed, and he looked with pleasure down at the straight creases in his trousers, at his neat patent leather boots with their suede tops. It pleased him tremendously to imagine himself once more properly "clothed and in his right mind."

The next thing would be a feed. He reminded himself of his hunger, and argued that he did not want anything "fancy." He would go to a grill and order just what he liked, and a lot of it. The "Trocerdilli" was just the place. First of all would come a "short one"—not that he needed an appetiser! He imagined himself seated at a table, the cloth startlingly white, the cutlery and glasses reflecting a thousand points of light. He could hear the band, above the whirr of conversation, playing something he knew. He was glancing down the menu card, and the waiter was at his side. A soup that was succulent, thick and hot—his mouth watered! Whitebait, perhaps. He saw their round little eyes and stiff tails as he squeezed his slice of lemon over them. He felt the wafer-slice of brown bread and butter in his fingers. A whisky-and-soda, and a double one at that, to drink—he was tired of these French wines. A *steak* "from the grill"—undoubtedly a steak—tender, juicy, red, with "chipped" potatoes, lying in long gold-and-brown fingers around it.

His teeth clashed at the thought of it! What would he have "to follow"? Something rich and cold! A *meringue glacée* was not good enough for the occasion. A cream *bombe glacée*, or, better still, a *Pêche Melba*. He saw the red syrup stuff in the little glass plate that it would be served on. And the peach—like the cheeks of a lovely child! At last, if he could manage it—which he did not at the moment doubt—something in the savoury omelette line. And to finish up with, the Egyptian should bring him some coffee. He saw the Egyptian very clearly, with his little red cap and his dusky cheeks. Then, last of all, the man with the cigars and liqueurs wheeled his tray. A good cigar from the top tray, clipped and lit by the man's lamp. Then to choose from the half score of bottles on the lower tray. Chartreuse, Benedictine, better still, Grand Marmier.

That really was all. Nothing to do now but lean back in his chair, and between his sips gaze contentedly through his cigar smoke at the lights, the mirrors, the palms, and whirring electric fans and the happy, flushed diners, with that curious, strained, puzzled and amused look that creeps into the backs of people's eyes at such times.

Then he pictured himself leaving the restaurant, climbing the stairs. The glass door was thrown open for him to pass through, with a gesture that was positively grandiloquent.

The cold air of the street was fanning his heated cheek. People were sweeping by him as he walked down Coventry Street. Ships that passed in the night! Passionate eyes stabbed him. Strange scents momentarily swept over him. . . .

There was a completeness of detail in all these pictures that wrung from him a very grim smile. Would he remember the war as vividly as he then remembered all that?

He saw himself pause in the gutter of Wardour Street while a taxi slid by. He saw himself survive the lure of the Empire, saw himself deciding not to cross the road, and go down to the Alhambra.

Eventually he reached a music hall. He was going in now. He was taking his place that moment in the plush stall. On the stage a little pseudo nigger was joking privately with the conductor. He laughed at one of the jokes he remembered. Then a woman came on. She was tragic, stately. He was thrilled by her slimness, her weirdness, her vitality. The whole atmosphere of the theatre was electrified by her personality. She was singing a song in a way that he had never heard before. He remembered it still. It was a Tango song. "His Tango girl!" His thoughts flew off at a tangent. . . .

CHAPTER 25

The Crossing of the Aisne

They spent a delectable night, with their boots off, between real blankets, after a real wash. Very early, before it was really light, they joined on to the battalion, and slid down the hill.

The subaltern had a few moments' talk with a friend who had commanded the "Divisional Guard" during the night.

"Scarcely got any sleep," he said. "But I took a peep at their room. It was laid out for a *pucca* breakfast. Jove, I could have done with some!"

At the door of the house he had been guarding, quite alone, and leaning heavily on his thick stick, stood the divisional commander. No doubt he knew of the struggle that lay before them, and was taking the opportunity of reviewing his battalions as they went in to battle. His face was red, his hair was iron grey, and rather long. He was a fine big man, there was a presence to him, a rugged and determined look.

A few minutes later they had plunged into the depths of a thick morning mist, that rolled like a lake between the heights. The steep road led them at length to the banks of the Aisne. The Germans had naturally blown up the bridge behind them, but the sappers had erected a temporary structure by the side of the ruined one. It quivered under their weight, and as the subaltern looked at the water swirling so swiftly beneath, he wondered what would happen if one of those huge shells were to blow it sky high. . . .

Running parallel to the river, and about thirty yards away, was a canal. This was likewise successfully passed, and so the Aisne was crossed without a shot being fired.

The battalion was concentrated while the rest of the brigade crossed the river. And all the time the sun was chasing away the light clouds of river vapour. Soon the enemy would see them, and they

101

would be caught in this difficult and dangerous movement, and the results would be disastrous.

But the minutes passed, and the mist melted almost entirely away, and still the guns were silent. At last they moved off, and began to ascend the slope. They were only just clear of the place when there was a whistle, a shriek, a bang and a roar. The explosion was two or three times greater than anything they had heard before. The very noise was intimidating, paralysing, and before they had had time to rally their nerves and collect themselves, before the awakened echoes had died away in the woods above, a second shell, as mighty as the first, sailed over their heads and exploded as titanically as it had done. This was the first occasion on which the British Armies had been brought face to face with the German super-heavy artillery. Naturally the result was a little disconcerting.

Tons of death-dealing metal and explosive were being hurled through the air as if Atlas were hurling stars about. There was something elemental, and superhuman about such colossal force. One felt like a pygmy in a Battle of the Gods.

They were profoundly ignorant of anything that was happening. Everything was normal, except the roar of guns. There was not even a sign of the cavalry being driven in. The only thing to do was to keep on until an order came, or something definite happened.

The road had turned into a village called Moussy, and was now running parallel to the river, along the side of the slope. An order was passed along to "keep down under cover of the right bank," so they advanced, half crouching, about half a mile.

Then, with a suddenness that amazed him, the subaltern saw the platoon in front begin to scramble hastily over the bank, and run off directly up the hill. No order was given, he could see no explanation for such a move. He hesitated for a second, wondering whether it would not be better to find out what was happening before he moved his platoon. But battles are sometimes lost by just such pauses, so he waved his arm, signalling to deploy and extend to the right. A second or so later his men were in line with the other platoon, advancing over a green field towards a bank. Their rifles were loaded, bayonets fixed, bodies bent forward—ready for anything.

They did not have long to wait.

Another "Jack Johnson" landed in front of them. They could see the earth as it flew upwards the other side of the hedge. Was it a chance shot, or would the Germans land a direct "hit" next time? That was the question that worried the subaltern as he advanced to the hedge. He was also puzzled as to what was really happening, or what he was expected to do. Not another officer was in sight.

In a few seconds the bank was reached. Here he made a temporary halt for the men to recover their breath. Men cannot be expected to shoot well if they cannot breathe.

Half a minute passed, and he began to consider the advisability of sending out several scouts to reconnoitre, as the whole responsibility of command in that part seemed to rest with him.

"'Ere's the captain a-comin' up," said a man.

Sure enough, there he was, coming up behind the bank. The subaltern heaved a sigh of relief.

"D'you know what this is all about, sir?"

"No," said the captain, as much as to say "How should I?"

"We had better hold on here, and wait and see what is to be done," he added.

Arm-chair strategists may not know it, but a man who has not learned how to "wait and see" is not much use in tactical warfare. War is not, as some people seem to think, an excuse for a perfect orgy of recklessness. But that is by the way.

"It would not be a bad idea if you went forward to see what is happening. I think I can see some people coming up between the trees on the left there."

The subaltern set out, without loss of time. Yes, there certainly were "people" advancing cautiously up the hill, from round the corner, but there were not many of them. Still crouching, he began once more to mount the hill. As he neared the top, he dropped on his hands and knees in the long grass, as he feared that he might unwittingly appear over the enemy's skyline, and be shot down where he stood.

He peered cautiously about him. The summit of the hill was round and smooth. Not a particle of cover was offered, but about twenty yards down the other side he saw the edge of a dense wood, which appeared to roll, uninterrupted, half-way up the further slope. The top of this slope formed the skyline, and seemed to be about three-quarters of a mile away. Except for the men working their way up on his left, whom he had already noticed, there was not a man in sight; but the shells were still sailing overhead.

At length the party came up, and amongst them was the colonel of one of the battalions in the brigade. The subaltern immediately asked him for orders.

"As far as I can see," said the colonel, "this hill is a sort of salient in our line. The enemy are probably holding that ridge along there," pointing to the skyline. "Anyway, we will hold on to this hill until I have orders for a general attack."

The subaltern walked down the hill to report what he had found out.

"All right," said the captain; "you had better take your platoon and all these men round about here, and help to hold on to the hill."

He called for his section commanders, explained what was to be done, and set off once more. As they were just about to cross the crest, he signalled to them to "get down," and at length they took up a sort of position along the edge of the wood on the other side.

The enemy had evidently not "spotted" them, and they were left in peace for an hour. Then their troubles began.

It seemed as though the hill suddenly became a place of vast importance. The colonel arrived upon the scene, with reinforcements of over a hundred men, and they immediately set to work putting the hill into a state of defence. Then a battery of field guns were drawn up into position on the "safe" side of the hill, and began without delay to shell the enemy. Their arrival, however, was decidedly a mixed blessing. So far, the troops had held the hill quite successfully, and had been undisturbed by hostile artillery, for the simple reason that the enemy was unaware of their positions. Now the artillery had come and "given the whole show away," and no sooner did the enemy discover that the hill was held, than he began forthwith to bombard them.

It was obviously impossible to continue "digging in." The only thing to do was to squeeze one's self into the ground, and pray. It seemed as if the titanic thunderbolts, that had hitherto been hurled aimlessly about, were suddenly concentrated on that one spot. It seemed as if all the gods in Olympus were hurling their rage upon it, determined to obliterate it from the face of the earth. The most gigantic guns that had ever been used in war were concentrating their fire upon it, and the result was awful. Nothing they had experienced before was comparable to it. It seemed as if the ground were being thrashed with whips of a thousand leaden-loaded thongs. The smell of the lyddite was nauseating, the uproar stupefying. Dust rose in the air; trees crashed to the ground.

Hell was let loose: Hell and Death were dashing around, converting that normal sky and that sane earth into a pandemonium. The wonder was that a human life was spared. The subaltern had a fleeting feeling that everyone except himself must be dead. When the storm seemed for a moment to have abated, he looked around him and was surprised to see that very little damage had been done to the men. An inexperienced eye would possibly not have detected any casualties at all. From a Kipling point of view, the scene was an artistic failure. Not a man was shrieking; not a man "clawing up the ground." Here and there men had rolled over on their sides, and were groaning quite softly to themselves. Here and there a purple patch in the dusty khaki. . . .

The instinct of men, like animals, is to crawl quietly away from their fellows, and die in solitude.

The colonel, very little perturbed by the bombardment, had sat throughout with his back resting against a tree, writing messages, or glaring at the map. Once, a large piece of shell casing had buried itself in the ground a few inches from his leg. The jagged piece was hot and heavy.

"Good Heavens," he said to himself, "what curious things *chance* and *fate* are. If I had stretched my leg out! Why didn't I?" He smiled.

At length a few stretcher bearers began to arrive, and the worst cases were carried off by them. Many of the less seriously wounded had to hobble, or even crawl down the hill, as best they could. It was a pitiable sight.

The subaltern looked up, and caught the eye of an officer being carried off on a stretcher. His mutilated leg was covered by his Burberry. He instantly recognised him as an officer who had "brought out" a "draft" some time previously.

If he were suffering great pain, he did not show it. He seemed annoyed, and a little ashamed.

"Just the look," thought the subaltern, "that a fellow wears when he's out at cricket—walking back to the pavilion."

The comparison, though not happy, was apt. It was just like cricket. Some missed their catches; some never had any sent to them; and others did brilliant things. A few had long innings, and compiled glorious scores, but the majority "got out" pretty soon.

He pulled from his pocket a "*Caporal*" cigarette, and placed it in his mouth, partly to show everyone around how cool this inferno had left him, and partly to steady his nerves. But just as he was striking the match, a violent desire to laugh assailed him. He suppressed this tendency towards hysterics, but he shook so much that it was impossible to light the cigarette, and in the end he threw it away in disgust.

And so the day dragged on. They were shelled with varying ferocity all the time. Once they attempted to launch an attack, but it failed, almost before it had started. The enemy artillery observation seemed too acute, the weight of his shells too heavy, and the wood in front too thick.

About three o'clock in the afternoon the general must have decided that the holding of the hill was too costly a business. He therefore ordered it to be evacuated, and the troops to retire on the village of Poussey. Everyone, from the colonel down, was privately relieved by this order, for every one felt that, if they had stayed there, by the end of the next day there would have been no regiment left.

The behaviour of the men had been superb. They had entered into this new phase of the war with that strange combination of recklessness and reliability which had made our "contemptible little army" what it was. Not a complaint had been uttered. They had joked all day—and there is an especial relish to jokes that are made between the thunderclaps—but they were worn out, not only by the terrors of that day, but by the accumulated loss of sleep and lack of food.

A further advance was impossible. The Germans had checked the onrush by the weight of their artillery. The victory of the Marne was over. The phase of the deadlock had begun.

CHAPTER 26

The Cellars of Poussey

The subaltern was too dazed to realise the significance of the day's fighting, but he brought his men back to the village without mishap, and behind the shelter of its walls they lay down to sleep just as they were.

In a little time the whole battalion was rallied in the village, and fresh reinforcements were sent forward to hold a line nearer the village.

The night that followed was cold and windy. In spite of a fire that his men lit in a little side street, and various sacks that they "lifted" from barns, the cold caused extreme discomfort, and it was with a great sigh of relief that at length dawn broke upon them.

The subaltern stumbled to his feet before it was fully light, shook the miserable sacks from his feet, and set out to explore the village.

Like most of its kind, it had only one central street, which was steep and winding. Underfoot were the usual cobbles, and the walls had a queer look of leaning inwards over the road with a protective air. He had not gone many yards before he came upon the little village square. Half of it was shut in by a huge, castle-like structure, which with its carved stone fountain gave the place almost a medieval air.

The gate in the wall was unlocked, and through the aperture he caught a glimpse of a trim garden and a comfortable-looking house.

"This," said the subaltern to himself, "is just the sort of place that the captain would choose for his headquarters."

He slipped into the garden and peeped through one of the windows. Sure enough, there were the captain, the senior subaltern and the doctor. They had already risen and were trying to boil a kettle on the ashes of last night's fire. It was not an inviting scene, by any means, but he pushed open the door, and started in the search for food.

The room in which he found them was a typical French kitchen, with a dirty grey ceiling, walls, and stone floor. The furniture consisted of a table, a couple of forms, and a chair or two. Otherwise there was absolutely no attempt at either comfort or adornment. Ransacking a dirty cupboard, the subaltern drew forth in triumph a promising-looking bottle, and having pulled the cork, smelt at the contents with caution. It contained a curious sort of liquor, apparently homemade, which saved their lives that morning. Then the doctor, after many amusing efforts to clean himself in a bucket, went off to the impro-vised hospital that had been set up in the village.

The early part of the morning passed peacefully enough; but the bombardment was renewed at about seven o'clock, and was followed by a hasty evacuation of the village to reinforce the front line. The captain's company, however, and one other, were ordered to stand by in reserve, but to be prepared to move at a moment's notice. The bombardment rolled on as usual for about an hour. Then came a tre-mendous crash, which made every wall and roof tremble, and gave warning that something worse than ordinary had happened.

Everybody rushed into the street, but there was no longer a square. One of the "Jack Johnsons" had alighted in the centre of it. The first glance at the scene disclosed the fact that the fountain had been blown sky high, and the cobbles torn up like pebbles, but it was not until afterwards that one realised that there had been men in that square. None was left alive in it now. One poor fellow had been struck by a piece of shell and had died before his head had crashed against the ground. The colour of the dead face reminded the subaltern haunt-ingly of the grey walls of the kitchen. Fortunately, the eyes were closed, but the horror of the thing—the shattered skull, the protrud-ing, blood-smeared brains, bit into the subaltern's soul. He gazed at it for a moment, spellbound, and then turned in towards the kitchen, feeling broken and humiliated.

"We must get them into better shelter than this," said the captain. "That might happen again."

The owners of the house came out to meet them. The old man and his wife seemed strangely unperturbed by the noise and the sights around them. He was a fine old man, with a yellow skin, long, flowing beard, and a bald head. He explained that he was the local mayor, and there was more natural dignity about him than many a lord mayor of a huge city. He told them that underneath his house was a cellar large enough to hide the whole company, and led the captain away to see it.

In a few moments they returned.

"Just the very place," said the captain; "we'll get the company down there right away, before the next big one comes over."

He led them down a flight of steps, opened a door, and stepped gingerly into pitch darkness. When their eyes became accustomed to the gloom, it was just possible to make out the dimensions of the place, and very gradually the men filed in, and lay down wherever they could. By the time the last man had pushed his way in, there was scarcely an unoccupied foot of room in the whole cellar.

After a time the talk died down, and sounds of slumber filled the darkness. Probably the only men in the whole company who did not spend the rest of that day in sleep were the "look-out" men, one posted in the road to intercept messages, and the other at the head of the steps to give warning.

As soon as it was dark they could leave the cellar with perfect safety—a thing they were glad to do, for the atmosphere was not as fresh as it might have been, and the place was very crowded. Only about half of the men, however, availed themselves of the opportunity. The others were too tired and just went on sleeping.

Sometime in the middle of the night they were awakened by the mess sergeant, who had successfully arrived with rations. The only possible way, it seemed, was to get supplies over the bridges under cover of darkness, as the enemy had got their range to a yard. He left their share of food, and then hurriedly left.

"If I don't get well over by the morning, I don't get over at all," he explained.

The next day was in every way similar to the previous one. No order to move was received, and sleep was the most popular occupation. Now and then, in intervals between the artillery duels, they would dash up the steps and air themselves as best as they could. In one of his rambles the subaltern alighted upon a peach tree, which was greatly appreciated. When the familiar sounds began again, they would troop once more down the steps and fall asleep in the cellar, until peace was restored.

On one occasion, following his men after he had seen them all safely down, a piece of high explosive shell-dust bounced from the wall, and embedded itself in the skin of his temple.

"By Jove!" he said, when he was safely in the cellar; "this is all very well, but if a big one did happen to drop on this house above here, we shouldn't stand the ghost of a chance. It would be better to be out in the open. We might be buried by the falling bricks."

Fate was kind. But once, on regaining the open, someone noticed that a weathercock had been struck off one of the gables.

"It just wanted to be twenty feet lower," said someone speculatively.

The subaltern enjoyed very much his short stay in Poussey. The old mayor and his wife were a charming couple, and as usual did everything in their power to make their Allies comfortable. On the other hand, it must be admitted that the British Officers, with their unfailing politeness and good spirits, made no small impression on them. The subaltern once heard the old lady say to her husband—

"*Eh! Mon vieux, quelle différence! Ils sont si gentils, si polis . . . et les autres . . . . Ach! Les cochons!*"

"What an impertinence," he thought, "to compare us!"

His coat was badly rent in the back, and once, while he was asleep, the old lady took it, and mended it with thick red twine.

Of course they had the inevitable sons or nephews at the front, and they had received no news of them. One had to listen with great attention, and an air of solicitude, and murmur some little consolations.

One morning, the subaltern forgets whether it was the first or second day of their stay, the old man took him into his library. It was a long, low room, fragrant with the smell of old books, and it looked out upon the leafy orchard. All the volumes were beautifully bound and nearly all were standard classics. He was surprised at the culture of this little spot, tucked away in the intellectual desert of rural France, and at the refinement of this man, who had been a farmer all his life. All the while a great battle was being fought outside; one could not be sure of life for a consecutive hour; at such a time it was amazing to be fingering fine old books, in the quiet, sombre library, by the side of an old man in a black velvet skullcap.

Eventually the subaltern picked out a volume by Ségur, not because he wanted to read about war, but because he feared that the Voltaires, the Rousseaux, and the Hugos would be too difficult for him. Ségur was easy: one could skip whole phrases without losing his gist: one was not worried by the words one did not know. He read of Napoleon's retreat on Paris—in its time accounted the most scientific retreat in history. Soissons! Montmirail! Why, they had almost passed into both these places! How everything that had ever happened would shrink before this—which was going on now, half a mile away.

CHAPTER 27

The First Trenches

Whether it was the second or third day of their stay in Poussey that the march began again the subaltern does not know. The only thing he remembers is being awakened from a peaceful afternoon nap, hurrying rather confusedly on parade, and marching off, out of the village. Turning sharply to the left, the troops descended the hill, and at length crossed the canal, which had evidently parted company with the Aisne. All was quiet, and he was making his way drowsily along the dusty road, when a whizz and a whistle brought him sharply to his senses. There could be no mistake about it, the shell was coming right at them.

"Oh, damn," he said; "we've been spotted."

The shell burst short of them.

There was a space of about two hundred yards that would obviously be shell swept, and the road offered not the slightest cover. Two hundred yards ahead there appeared to be a good stout bank, which would shield them very effectually. The only thing to be done was to rush on as fast as they could, and thus suffer as few casualties as possible.

The men, however, did not quite realise the situation. By long training and a great deal of actual experience they had learned that the best thing to do when you are under fire is to tear for the nearest cover, and, failing that, flop down on your faces where you stand, and take your chance. As a general rule this proved sound enough, but in this especial case it was obvious to the officers that the longer they delayed, the heavier would be the casualty list, a fact which the men did not understand. The British soldier is a sportsman, and understands the game as well as his officer. He only wants to be led; and in battle, scarcely that. Driving is an art absolutely unknown in the

British Army.

In the stress of the tense moments that followed, the subaltern owned to himself that as a driver he was not much good. The German artillery had got their range to a yard, and it was very trying to have to stand up in the open and spend precious seconds in urging on men who ought to have known better. He was strongly tempted to run for it, but a sense of duty prevailed, and he stayed there dashing about in a futile effort to speed matters up. He shouted, he shrieked, he swore, he has a dim recollection of even kicking at his men in the effort to get on out of the terrible danger zone. But perhaps to his overwrought nerves the delay seemed longer than perhaps it really was, or perhaps force of numbers from behind succeeded where he had failed; anyhow, he got his platoon into safety, and only sustained the loss of five or six men.

His platoon sergeant behaved with an intrepid bravery that gave him a moral right to the Victoria Cross. He stayed in the fire-swept area to carry two wounded men into safety, and tended several others as they lay. He received no recognition—but those who were near him will never forget.

The bank reached, safety was achieved for the moment, at any rate. They pushed on for another half-mile or so, and were then halted under cover of the bank. They had not long to wait before the purpose of the whole manoeuvre was revealed to them. In their capacity of local reserve they had been hurried to the point of the line where the next attack in force was expected.

The whole thing was ridiculous in its mechanical exactitude. In about five minutes the artillery bombardment died down. Hard upon its heels arose a most lively rifle-fire, which showed clearly enough that the preparatory bombardment was over, and the real attack about to begin. Higher and higher rose the note struck by the rifle-fire, as the contest thickened. Never had they heard such intensity of concentration before. Now up, now down, it rocked on in one sweeping, continuous note for nearly half-an-hour. Then it died down, almost to silence. The attack had failed, and the local reserve would not be needed.

It does not require much imagination to picture the state of mind of the men in reserve—cowering behind the bank. They could almost see the whole thing—the grey dots crawling over the crest of the hill, the shots that announced their detection, the uprising of them in a solid mass, sweeping towards the trenches; the withering fire, reaping in its victims like a scythe. They were wondering every second of the time, "How far have the Germans got? Have they pushed us out?" But no order came to advance to recapture the trenches, so they presumed all was well.

As the crossing of the open ground had been so rough, they were allowed to postpone their return journey until it was dark. But even then they were not safe.

The colonel led the battalion a clear two hundred yards away from the road. The darkness was so intense that they could not be seen, but in the silence of the night they were sure to be heard, and, on hearing them, the Germans would certainly plaster the road with shells in the hope of "getting" them as they returned.

The colonel was right. The German observation-posts must have heard them, for the old, familiar whizz came whistling through the darkness. The first shells seemed incredibly long in the air. One's heart was in one's mouth, as one listened to hear if they were going "to fall short," or "go over." Then the crash came, in front, on the road, and they knew that the colonel had saved them once more. Even as it was, their company quartermaster-sergeant was hit in the foot.

The shelling in the darkness must have affected the nerves of the leading company. They struck out at a tremendous pace. The subaltern was dropping further and further behind. He could not keep up, and the prospect of losing touch in the darkness was extremely serious.

At last the canal bridge was reached and the bombardment ceased, but instead of being allowed to turn in towards Poussey, they were told to relieve the other two companies in the trenches.

They found the line, and "took over" the trenches without mishap. Of course, in those days trenches were not built as they were later. To begin with, the men had no tools, except their "entrenching implements," so naturally the work could not be very elaborate. Moreover, the thought that such works would be wanted for longer than a day or two never entered their heads. Each man dug a shelter for himself, according to his skill, ingenuity and perseverance. There was little or no attempt at digging a long, consecutive trench. A series of holes had been dug, that was all.

The monotony of the night was broken by the arrival and distribution of rations. An hour or so after this had been accomplished the east began to grow grey, and they were soon able to take stock of their surroundings.

The trenches, or rather holes, were dug on the side of the road. Behind them the ground sloped straight down to the canal. They could not actually see the enemy trenches; and there was no attempt made by either side to "snipe."

The first day of trench life—if such it could be called—was not a very trying experience. There was nothing to do except a little improvement of the shelters. Their only duty was to "wait and see." It was not cold, and they had their rations. The subaltern dug, and slept, and ate, and then dug again, and thus the day passed. Indeed, he even began to write a long letter home in his notebook, but he lost the pages almost as soon as they were written.

They were shelled twice during the day, but all one had to do was to lie comfortably in one's "funk hole" and wait for the "hate" to die down. After many experiences in the open, without a particle of cover, being shelled in deep holes had few terrors.

"Of course," he said to himself, "if they get a direct hit on this hole I'm done for, but otherwise I'm pretty safe."

Nevertheless, in spite of the holes, several men were carried away.

The greatest inconvenience to the place was the stench of decaying horses. About twenty yards down the hill the horses belonging to a whole battery had been struck by a shell. About a dozen of them lay dead where they had been standing. The story had been told of how one of the subalterns of the other company had left his hole, rifle in hand, in the middle of a bombardment, to put the wounded animals out of their agony. He had succeeded in shooting them all, but on his way back had been struck in the foot with a piece of shell casing. It was an heroic, kindly act, typical of the brave man who did it. But it seemed a pity. . . .

It was, of course, impossible to bury the dead animals, and to drag them further away was out of the question in the daylight. There was nothing else to do but to sit tight and endure in silence.

Their second night in the trenches was merely a repetition of the first. After a lively sunset fusillade had died down, the Germans lay quiet until dawn. The German artillery were so regular in their habits that it almost seemed as though they must be working by a printed programme, which directed that at six o'clock precisely in the morning, every battery was to fire off a certain number of rounds, absolutely regardless of whatever targets they might have been offered, and, having fired the requisite number of rounds, the battery was to lie quiet until, say, eleven o'clock. Of course, the thing was ludicrous, but it seemed to be the only explanation.

A mail was included in the rations. He himself drew blank, but the senior subaltern was sent a box of chocolates. The sight of them, on active service, was a farce. They were not the usual sort of chocolates that one saw—"plain," useful, nourishing chocolates. They were frankly fancy chocolates, creams with sugared tops, filled with nuts, marzipan, or jellies, inseparable from a drawing-room, and therefore ten times more acceptable and delightful.

He got not a single letter from home, not from any one. Not that he minded much, at that time. Home, parents—any softness of any description—would have seemed unreal.

The happiness of the following day was very much impaired by rain, which fell intermittently throughout the whole day. After the first shower he got up and began to look about him for some sort of protection. Rather than have nothing, he picked up a waterproof sheet that had belonged to a wounded man. It was covered with blood, but the next shower soon washed all trace of it off, and it kept him dry.

The next night, just after rations had been distributed, an order came to march off. Haste, it seemed, was imperative. And so, leaving behind as few things as possible, he paraded his men, without knowing where they were to go, and saw them set off behind the front platoon. Just as he was about to set off himself, he slipped down the side of one of the holes, and as he fled, his sword slid from its scabbard, and vanished. He knew the chances of returning to that particular spot were five to one against, and he was determined to "hang on" to his sword, come what might, so he let his platoon go on, while he groped about in the darkness for it. It seemed incredible that a sword could hide itself so completely. He kicked about in the pitch-dark for what seemed to be endless minutes before his foot knocked against it. He "pushed it home" hurriedly, and started off in pursuit of the men.

But the darkness had swallowed them up. He followed the road right into Poussey, but still there was no sign of them. No troops, he learned, had passed through since the previous morning. Evidently they had not gone that way. The only alternative was the "awkward" road over the canal bridge which led into the next village on the line—Souvir.

CHAPTER 28

In Reserve at Souvir

He hurried on, for morning would break in half-an-hour, and he did not wish to be caught in that unwholesome hundred yards the other side of the canal bridge. He overtook his men sooner than he expected, and the open space was passed without any resistance.

"They're probably expecting a big attack at dawn, and they've brought us up in reserve again," someone said.

Sure enough, the attack took place, but, like its predecessor, it failed, and they naturally expected to be sent back to the trenches at Poussey. In this, however, they were disappointed. Dawn having broken, it was apparently thought to be needlessly imprudent to make the battalion run the gauntlet once again. So they were allowed to stay where they were, with the caution that they were to be ready to move within five minutes of the colonel's receipt of the order. It may sound a long time, but only a smart and efficient battalion can do it. The adjutant has to open and acquaint the C.O. of the order. He has to rap out his own orders. Sleeping men have to be roused, equipment thrown on, arms taken up. The men have to "fall in" in their right sections; have to be numbered, have to form fours. If there is any muddle whatever, a battalion cannot move off in five minutes.

They slept propped up against the bank for some hours; then they were moved further up the road into the little village of Souvir. It appeared that their new *rôle* was to act as local reserve, and that they could amuse themselves how they liked as long as they were prepared "to move off at fifteen minutes' notice."

The men broke into two big barns and made themselves tolerably comfortable. They lit little fires in the road and began to cook their breakfasts. The officers of the company billeted themselves on the hovel nearest the barns and set about the same object.

"I think," mused the senior subaltern, "that it would be an excellent idea if some of us went on a foraging expedition. I should not be at all surprised if we did not have to stop here for weeks. And there may be one or two things to be picked up—before the others."

So two of them went off on a tour of inspection. Noticing beehives outside the house of the village priest, they went in and bought two large jars of liquid honey. An *estaminet* yielded a couple of bottles of Médoc, and a *pâtisserie*, most unexpectedly, some bread.

Having successfully settled their business, there was time to look around. Souvir was a bigger village than Poussey, and seemed to be teeming with troops, who looked as if they had been used to the place for years, and were likely to remain in it longer. The first object of interest was the church, which had been turned into a hospital for Germans, many of whom were sitting about on benches in the stone-flagged courtyard. The two officers went in to have a closer look at them. The majority were so greyish pale, their hair such unlovely stubble, their temples so shrunken that the subaltern pitied them in their morose dejection and slow-witted taciturnity.

"I don't think we'd better go into the church," he said. "They'd probably throw us out."

They passed through an archway in a huge medieval wall into the graveyard, and thence, by a sudden and complete transformation in time, colour and atmosphere, into a most delightful garden of magnificent proportions, with smooth lawns and sweeping drives. The *château* itself was scarcely in keeping with this stateliness. The impression it gave one came as an anti-climax. The subaltern was beginning to develop a fine taste in French *châteaux*, but somehow this one did not rank with the others, although his brain reeled at the thought of the cost of it all. Probably that is why it failed as a work of art and beauty: it made one wonder how much it must have cost.

A passer-by told them that it belonged to a certain woman whose name had been on everybody's lips, just before the war, and the information stimulated their interest. They wandered around, past silent fountains and over velvet lawns, stone terraces and gravel drives. On their way back they passed one of the big bay windows on the ground floor of the *château*. It was open, and they caught the faint but distinctive aroma of disinfectant. The erstwhile billiard-room had obviously been converted into a hospital dressing-room. The place was deserted, and they turned away without the intuition entering into either of their heads that they themselves would before long be carried into that very room.

Souvir was apparently their headquarters for the time being, for if they moved away by day or night, they always marched back into it. And as, day by day, they saw the same sights and did the same things, the passage of time did not leave such exact impressions on his mind as the changing sights and actions of the moving battles had done.

Compared with the days that had gone before they were divinely comfortable. Unless there was an alarm, they could sleep as long as they liked. There was not sufficient accommodation in the little hut, so the officers commandeered a little shed at the side of it. Here there was plenty of straw, and for several mornings they lay dozing until eight or nine o'clock.

The men were quite happy in their barns, and would not begin to stir before seven o'clock. Then they would hear in their sleep confused sounds of tramping feet and shouts in the road outside.

The voice of the quartermaster-sergeant, distributing the rations, was always the most insistent.

"'*Ere*, who's 'ad that there tea?"

"Forty-two Smith took it down the street, Cooler Sawgint."

(When there is more than one man of the same name in a Battalion, the last two figures of his regimental number, are, as it were, hyphenated on to it. Brown's number was, say, 1965, so to prevent mistakes he was always '65 Brown, to distinguish him from all the other Browns.)

"Where's the orderly cor'pril of No. 5 Platoon?"

"Comin', Cooler Sawgint!"

Then another voice raised in pained expostulation—

"'*Ere*, look at '*im*—a hackin' up the bacon. Who d'ju think's comin' after you?"

"Go and see why there ain't no rum, Watkins!"

"There ain't '*arf* enough sugar for all them!"

"'And over my firewood, will ye, or I'll . . . !"

And so on, and so forth. It was the tune to which they finally awoke every morning.

When it was impossible to maintain the pretence of being asleep any longer, they would get up and shake themselves. They had passed the stage of wanting to take clothes off. Their uprising in the morning was as easy and simple as a dog's. Then, aided, perhaps, by one of their servants, they would set about getting their breakfast ready in the front room. The subaltern discovered what a tremendous amount of trouble is entailed in the preparation of even the simplest meals. Tables to be moved, kettles to be filled, bread cut, jam and bully beef tins opened! But each would have his own particular job, and they would soon be seated round the dirty table, drinking their tea out of cups, or their own mugs, and munching biscuits or bread.

Now that they were getting their rations each night with the regularity of clockwork, they were beginning to appreciate properly the excellence of their fare. "Seeing," as the senior subaltern would say, "that we are on active service, I think the rations is an extraordinarily well managed show."

The quality was good, and there was plenty of it. Personally, the subaltern never succeeded in getting on very good terms with the "bully beef." He decided that it was "a bit too strong" for him; but the others devoured large quantities, and seemed all the better for it.

The jam, at that time, and in that particular sector of the line, was good and, moreover, varied. The subaltern does not ever remember suffering from the now notorious "plum and apple." There was even marmalade.

He openly delighted in the biscuits, and would go about his work all day munching them. The bacon, too, as someone said, was "better than what we have in the mess, sometimes." None of them posed as connoisseurs of rum, but a sergeant, who looked as if he knew what he was talking about, praised it heartily; and, taken in hot tea, it banished all sorts of cares. . . .

Tea (without rum) and bacon, to be followed by ration bread and marmalade (if possible) was the staple fare at breakfast. They would sit around the fire and smoke—there was a tobacco allowance included in the rations. The subaltern, however, had lost his pipe, and attempts at cigarette rolling were not particularly successful.

Every other day there used to be a mail, and with it, generally, papers from home. This was the first definite news they had had from "home" since leaving in mid-August. There was an enthralling interest in seeing how the people at home "were taking things."

To be perfectly candid, before the war, the army had placed very little reliance upon the patriotism or integrity of the country. The army was a thing apart—detached from the swirl of conflicting ideas, and the eddies of political strife. The army was, so to speak, on the bank, and it looked with stern disapproval at the river sweeping so swiftly by. It neither understood the forces that were hurrying the waters along, nor did it realise the goal that they were striving to reach.

Perhaps it did not take the trouble, perhaps it could not.

Then, when the war clouds began to blacken the horizon, the army, having so little sympathy with the vast and complex civilisation which it was to defend, felt convinced that the national feelings and political sense of the nation would be slumbering so soundly that no call of honour could awaken it to the realisation of either its duty or its danger. But the horse which all the expert trainers had dismissed as a "non-starter" for the next great race, suddenly gathered his haunches under him, and shot out on the long track to victory. The army, with the rest of the world, realised that, after all, the heart of the nation was in the right place. Nevertheless, the tremendous wave of patriotism that had swept so splendidly over Britain caused, at first, not a little suspense.

"Good Heavens! he's asking for a million men," gasped the subaltern.

"Well, if he doesn't get them, this company will go over and fight for Germany," said the captain. "The country isn't worth fighting for if it can't raise a million men."

"The government seem to be doing jolly well," someone volunteered.

"And so they darn well ought," said the senior subaltern. "But you wait and see. If something wonderful does not happen in about six months' time, all sorts of fools will be up on their hind legs, shouting out how the show, as they would do it, should be run."

As events turned out, the senior subaltern was not far wrong.

At this time, too, the country was thrilled with its first feeling of pride in the army since Waterloo. The dramatic rush of events—Mons, the Retreat, the dramatic rally when all seemed lost, and the splendid victory of the Marne, the continued advance, the deadlock on the Aisne—people were gasping at the magnificence of the success. They realised that the swift and sudden victory which Germany had counted on had been frustrated, and that owing to the French and the "contemptible little army" eventual victory had been assured.

Everyone who had the ear of the "public" was raining praise upon this contemptible little army, and the contemptible little army was surprised; but although they classified the eloquent speeches and dashing articles under the sweeping phrase of "hot air," these things pleased them a good deal, although they never have admitted it. The country, it appeared, had learned to appreciate them—a little late, it is true; still, in the volatile imagination of the public, they had arrived. They were quietly pleased, and awoke to the realisation of what fine fellows they were.

"No more of the 'expensive, idle loafer' talk," said someone.

It was the vindication of the British Army.

CHAPTER 29

To Straighten the Line

Later in the morning there would probably be an inspection of arms. They had always to be very careful that the rifles were in proper working order. A few stiff bolts at a critical moment might make all the difference.

The next function would be dinner. This generally consisted of bully beef made into a sort of stew, and some potatoes, stolen from a field nearby. It must be confessed that the stews were not a great success, and the subaltern conceived a violent dislike to them. The sudden change from "the move" to "reserve" perhaps upset his system. He confessed to not "feeling very fit." The others, however, all seemed to have insatiable appetites for food and sleep. Instead of marching twenty miles a day on one or two meals, they now had their rations regularly and got very little exercise. They slept as if sleeping sickness was laying its hold upon them, and when not sleeping they were eating.

The wine store had not yet been exhausted in the village, and very often they had a bottle with their suppers. The honey in the two jars seemed inexhaustible—indeed, everybody grew tired of it in time; and in the end the remnants were presented to another company. The *pâtisserie* continued to yield new bread, and they ate such quantities of it, still hot from the oven, that many of them got "livers." They were notoriously the first company when it came to "looking after themselves." "Which," as the senior subaltern said, "shows sense."

Once, when they had just finished their midday meal, the usual order "to stand to arms" came through, and they were hurried along the road that ran parallel to the river, towards Soissons. The march was longer than usual, and they were just beginning to entertain hopes that the deadlock had been broken and that they were once more on the advance, when an abrupt halt was called, and they were ordered to throw themselves hastily behind the bank along the roadside.

They could see nothing, neither friend nor foe. The only sound of firing was miles and miles down the line, in the direction of Poussey. The subaltern's platoon happened to be the second in the leading company. Already there was movement in front, and, crawling forward to the end of the line, he climbed up the bank to take stock of the position. To the north was a little copse, the intervening ground a vegetable field. Further off, to the east, there was a big hill, crowned with a dense-looking forest which, as far as he could see, was deserted.

The colonel, who was not to be deceived by a new appearance of quietude, had somehow made his way to the little copse, and was examining the hill with his glasses. The adjutant, who had followed him, presently rose to his feet.

"Bring . . . your . . . men . . . over . . . carefully . . . in . . . extended . . . order!"

The words floated across on the wind.

Feeling that he would like to see his men all safely across before he left any of them, the subaltern motioned to the sergeant to lead them, and they set off in a long, dotted and irregular line towards the thicket.

"Hurry . . . them . . . up. Hurry!" shouted the adjutant.

And just as the last man had left the bank, and he had started himself, he realised what the adjutant meant.

"*Phwhizz . . . phwizz . . . phwizz.*"

Like malignant wasps the bullets hummed past him. There was a regularity in the discharge and a similarity in the aim that left him no chance to doubt that a machine-gun had been turned on them.

"I was a bit of a fool not to have gone first," he said to himself.

But the bullets hummed harmlessly by his head and shoulders, and the thought that struck him most forcibly, as he plunged through the cabbages, was the impossibility of realising the consequences if any one of them had been a few inches nearer his head. It momentarily occurred to him to lie down and crawl through the cabbages, trusting to luck that the machine-gun would lose him; but, of course, the only thing was to run for it, and so he ploughed along. Whether the journey occupied more than a minute or not he is unable to say, but it seemed an incredible lapse of time before he reached the copse—and safety.

"We shall have some artillery turned on to us in a minute," said the colonel; "we had better get on with the operation."

They debouched from the copse in open order, and advanced in the usual lines of platoons, to attack the hill.

The subaltern loosened his sword in his scabbard, so that when the time came he could draw it more easily. He had already picked up a rifle from some unfortunate.

There seemed to be a certainty of a hand-to-hand fight. He did not feel at all eager to kill; on the other hand, he scarcely felt afraid. He just felt as if he grudged the passing of the yards under his feet which separated him from the edge of the wood. The idea of being "stuck" himself never occurred to him.

The bullets flew about rather thickly for the first few minutes, but no harm was done, and then the enemy's resistance seemed to die down. There was complete silence for several minutes as our men plodded steadily on. Then, away on the right, the colonel's whistle sounded, and a halt was called.

The enemy had taken fright and had retired, machine-guns and all, before their advance.

This little affair, although too small to figure in the communiqués at home, was a great personal triumph for the colonel. The enemy, having broken through the line and pushed his way almost to the banks of the river, had been driven back and the line straightened out, without, as far as the subaltern could see, any loss whatever.

They were not allowed to follow up this easy success, and consequently the enemy was still left in possession of a small salient. The subaltern's own company was then sent to prolong the right of the battalion, and to get in touch with the "people" on the right.

This was eventually done; the "people" proving to be a regiment of cavalry, employed as infantry.

In this particular part of the line the situation was, to say the least of it, a little muddled. The cavalry did not seem to be altogether at home in their new rôle. Their trenches seemed too small and detached. The front was covered with copses, which were continually changing hands. The whole line seemed to be dangerously weak, and the facilities for communication too precarious. The subaltern regarded the whole affair as a sort of nightmare, and prayed fervently that they would not be made to stop permanently in that quarter.

It appeared that they had been told off to hold in check the side of the salient. They took up their position along the edge of a wood, three or four yards in it.

"We'll be shelled in about twenty minutes, so dig all you know," said the captain.

How they dug can be easily understood. They had only their entrenching implements, but in ten minutes most of them had very fair "lying down" cover. Ten minutes was all they were allowed. There was no artillery fire by the end of that time, but the bullets began to whizz past, or flatten themselves in the tree trunks. It was rather hard to see precisely what was happening. Black dots emerged from the wood, and quickly flitted back again. The enemy seemed rather half-hearted.

When the attack, if attack it could really be called, had subsided, a sergeant got up from somewhere down the line, and continued work on his hole. There was a whizz overhead, and he dropped back abruptly. The subaltern thought that he had realised the danger and had naturally bobbed down for safety, but word was passed up "to keep down, as Sergeant Simkins had been shot dead—through the heart." He never uttered a sound, and must have met his death instantly.

Work was continued, but with the utmost caution. Meanwhile the afternoon was drawing rapidly to a close, and the prospect of holding such a position appalled the subaltern when he thought of it. The sergeant had been killed by enfilade fire. It was quite obvious that their line was thrown out, as it were, between the two general lines. Consequently they were enfiladed by the enemy, threatened very seriously on their front, on account of the proximity of the copses, and if forced to retire there was absolute certainty of being mown down by their own cavalry. The senior subaltern succeeded in clearing one copse, after firing a few shots and making a bold advance, but had not sufficient men to retain it. Then, just as darkness was closing down on the hopeless tangle, a message was passed up to "close on the road."

The relief at this order was impossible to describe. Their spirits rose meteorically. They scarcely succeeded in hiding their joy from the cavalry who were to be left in their trenches, and when they set off towards Poussey there was a wonderful swing in their step.

In an hour's time they were back in their old billets, and the officers opened a bottle of wine, on the strength, as someone said, of getting out of an "extraordinarily awkward position."

"Well," said the captain, with a half-full tumbler in his hand, "here's hoping that our wonderful luck keeps in."

They drank in silence, and soon after adjourned to the outhouse.

CHAPTER 30

The Jaws of Death

The next morning they learned that their turn of duty as local reserve was over, and that they were "to take over" a line of trenches that evening. The captain went alone to be shown round in the morning.

They wrote letters all morning, had an early dinner, and retired early to the outhouse to put in a few hours sound sleep in anticipation of several "trying" nights.

At about five o'clock they awoke, and found that the captain had returned in the meantime. He explained the position to them as they drank their tea.

"The trenches are just in the edge of a wood," he said. "It is extraordinarily thick. It would be absolutely impossible to retire. The field of fire is perfect. The skyline is only two hundred yards away, and there wouldn't be an inch of cover for them, except a few dead cows."

"I shouldn't think dead cows were bullet-proof, should you?" asked the senior subaltern.

"There's one thing you will have to watch. There are any amount of spies about, and they let the Germans know, somehow, when the reliefs are coming up the road, and then the road gets searched. They don't know exactly where you are, you see. They have the road on the map, and plaster it on the off chance. If you see a shell burst on the road, the only thing to do is to get clear of it. Give it about forty yards' grace, and you will be safe enough."

Soon after they set out along a road that they had never travelled before, leading directly up the hill in front of Souvir. About half-way up, they almost stumbled into the holes that the German shells had eaten deep into the road. Evidently, however, the spies in Souvir had not succeeded in informing the enemy of their approach. There was perfect quietness.

It was a stiff hill to climb, and they halted alongside of a battery of artillery to take breath. There was a deep cave in the rock, which the gunners had turned into a very comfortable "dug-out." The subaltern envied them very sincerely. He felt he would have given anything to have been a "gunner." They had such comfortable dug-outs—horses to ride—carriages to keep coats and things in. Above all, there could not be that terrible strain of waiting—waiting.

The road curled sharply round the rock precipice, and plunged into a thick forest. A guide had met them, and absolute silence was ordered. They had breasted the rise, and were nearing the trenches. The road had ceased abruptly, and the paths that they had laboured along were nothing but narrow canals of mud. Here and there a few broken trees and mangled branches showed where a shell had burst.

Hands were held up silently in front. A halt was ordered for a few minutes, while the leading platoon moved along into its allotted trenches. They had arrived.

Nothing warned the subaltern, when at length he was shown the line for his own platoon, that this night was to be any different from any of the other nights he had spent in the face of the enemy.

It was not, strictly speaking, a line of trenches at all. As usual, each man had dug a hole by himself, and each man was his own architect. Very few holes had been connected by a rough sort of trench at the back. The captain had described the topography of the situation very exactly. The holes were dug on the borders of the forest, but were concealed from enemy artillery observation by the trees. The field of fire was absolutely open. It stretched to the top of the hill, which formed their horizon, a distance of rather less than two hundred yards. It was smooth grass, and it struck the subaltern as being exceptionally green. A few dead cows, in the usual grotesque attitudes of animals in death, were scattered over the green grass.

He selected his hole, and then began to take careful stock of his surroundings. The fact that he could see no sign of the opposite trenches perhaps lulled him into a sense of false security. Anyway, after having disposed of his haversack, and the sacks he had brought up with him, he got up from his hole, and began to walk along behind the holes. On the extreme left he found his sergeant.

"Well, this looks a pretty safe position," he said.

"Yes, sir. I've just had a shot at a man's head that I thought I saw out there. I can't say whether or no I shot him. He disappeared quick enough. I should put the range at two hundred and fifty, sir."

"I wonder what is on our left, here?" he asked.

"I don't know, sir. I haven't had time to look."

"I think I had better go and find out for myself."

He set off, pursuing his way through the thick undergrowth and trees. It was longer than he thought. But all was still quiet, so the thought of being "spotted" in the open did not occur to him.

He found the edge of the next trench. It was thrown forward in front of the wood. After making the usual arrangements that are vaguely called "establishing touch," he turned back out of the shelter of the parapet, over the dangerous ground.

Twilight was deepening every second. He did not run; and he only hurried, because he wanted to get really established in his "funk hole" before it grew too dark to see what he was doing.

Then, almost simultaneously, the enemy and the regiment in the trenches opened fire. He stopped short, and turned round to watch. He could see nothing but thin red spurts of fire in the grey twilight. He turned quickly on his heel, meaning to reach his own men before the attack should develop on their front, where, as yet, all was quiet.

He almost reached the end of his trenches. . . .

★★★★★★

There was a crisp crash, a blinding light flew up like a circular sun-set around him, a dreadful twinge, as of hair and skin and skull being jerked from his head with the strength of a giant! For the millionth part of a second he was at a loss to understand what had happened. Then, with sickening horror, he realised that he had been shot in the head.

It is impossible to convey with what speed impressions rushed through his mind.

The flaring horizon tilted suddenly from horizontal nearly to per-pendicular. His head rushed through half a world of black, fury-space. His toes and finger-tips were infinite miles behind. A sound of rush-ing waters filled his ears, like deathly waterfalls stamping the life from his bursting head. Black blurred figures, nebulous and meaningless, loomed up before his face.

"Hit in the head—you're done for."

"Hit in the head—you're done for."

The inadequate thought chased through his brain.

"What a pity, what a shame; you might have been so happy, later on."

"What a pity, what a shame; you might have been so happy later on."

He was conscious that it was a foolishly futile thought at a supreme moment.

His life seemed pouring out of his head, his vitality was running down as a motor engine, suddenly cut off. He felt death descending upon him with appalling swiftness. Where would the world go to? And what next?

He was afraid.

Then, with a tremendous effort he turned his thoughts on God, and waited for death.

He was swimming in that black fury-sea that was neither wet nor clinging. He was made of lead in a universe that weighed nothing. He was sinking, sinking. In vain he struggled. The dark, dry waters closed over him. . . .

★★★★★★

Still the waterfalls pounded in his ears, and still the dry waves reeled before his eyes, and under his head a pool, sticky and warm.

What was that? This time surely something tangible and real moving towards him. With a supreme effort he tried to jerk his body into moving. His left leg moved. It moved wearily; but still it moved. His left arm too.

What was this?

The right arm and leg were gone, gone.

The rest of him was flabbergasted at the horror of the discovery.

No, not gone! They were there. But they would not move. He could not even *try* to move them. He could not so much as *feel* them.

Then he awoke to the horror of the thing.

His right side was dead!

★★★★★★

The shape was really alive. It resolved itself into a man crawling in the darkness to his rescue.

"You need not bother about me, I'm done for. Get back into the trench."

He had a feeling that though he meant his lips to frame these words, he was in reality saying something quite different. It was an exhausting effort to speak.

The form asked him questions in a fierce whisper. He had not the strength to understand or answer.

Very slowly and cautiously he was dragged over the few yards of ground that separated him from the first hole.

It was awful. His brain conceived the thought: "For God's sake let me die in peace." But his lips were all twisted, and refused to move at the bidding of his brain. He could only groan.

With wonderful gentleness the man placed his officer's broken head over the hole, and with the help of another man lowered him into it.

His next thought was: "Well, they can only hit my feet, now!" There had not been room in the hole for all of him, so his feet had been left protruding out of it. The thought fanned some smouldering ember of humour in him. A moment later he discovered with a thrill—

"I'm going to live, I'm going to live. I *will* live!"

The discovery, and the resolution which followed, by no means excited him. He arrived quite quietly at the conclusion. And set his mind to await the development of the next event.

The man who had dragged him in now tied the "first field dressing" over his head, and fastened the strings beneath his chin. Interminable ages passed slowly by, and yet the doctor did not come. He regarded the arrival of the doctor, like the coming of the Last Day, as the end of all difficulties, and the solution of many mysteries.

Needless to say he was disappointed. The doctor could naturally do little or nothing for him. With the aid of a match or two he "had a look," replaced the dressing by some bandages, and moved him about a little to ease his position. To carry him away that night, said the doctor, was absolutely impossible. And with that he went away.

The senior subaltern, who had come up with him, stayed a little longer, and earned his eternal gratitude. He made further efforts to straighten him out, assured him that the effects of the shock would wear off by morning, and that he would once more be able to move. He collected a few extra blankets and coats and spread them over him, for he was growing terribly cold. Then with cheery words on his lips he left him.

Left alone in the silence of the night, the subaltern felt the horror of the situation take hold of him. He was alone with his pain and his paralysis. There was no hope of alleviation until morning. What time was it then? he asked himself. Seven, at the latest. That meant eight long hours of agony, before anything *happened*! That is what the wounded love and long for—something to happen—something to distract the attention from the slow, insistent pain—something to liven drooping spirits, and raise falling hopes.

Slowly and surely he began to take stock of the situation. First of all came his head. The pain of the wound was an ache, a dull ache that sharpened into shooting pains if he moved. Still, he told himself that it might be worse. There was much worse pain in the world. It could not be called unbearable or excruciating.

His spine seemed in some way twisted. It ached with an insistence and annoyance only second to the wound. All his most determined efforts to wriggle it straight failed lamentably. Indeed, he almost fancied that they made matters worse.

As for the paralysed limbs, theirs was a negative trouble. He did not know where his right hand was. He had to grope about with his left hand under coats to find it. And when found, it was as if he had grasped somebody else's hand. The situation was weird, and in an uncanny way it amused and pleased him to take hold of the inert fingers. They were so soft and cold. The hand of a dead man, heavy, heavy—impossible to describe the dragging, inert weight of it.

But what frightened him more than anything was his face. One side was drawn up, and was as impossible to move as the arm. The lower jaw seemed clamped to the upper, and it, too, ached. A horrible fear crept into his head.

"Tetanus!"

He recalled tales of the terrible end of those who were marked down by this terrible disease. How they died in awful agony, the spine bent backwards like a bridge!

In spite of the coats, the cold seemed to eat into his very heart.

He started the night bravely enough, and fought against his troubles until his nerve collapsed hopelessly. The night was too long: it was too much to bear. He groaned aloud in his agony, and discovered that it was an immense relief.

The men near him began to open fire. If it were really an attack, it was soon beaten down, and he began to shriek at them for wasting precious ammunition that they might want when it was too late. He used words that he never even knew that he knew. Great bursts of anger, he found, distracted his attention from the pain, if only for a few moments. To this end he worked himself into such a transport that the bleeding recommenced, and he was forced to cease, exhausted. In another hour his nervous downfall was completed. He began to cry.

Each second of the interminable night dragged slowly by, as if it gloated over his pain. In the end it became too much for him and he fainted away, peacefully and thankfully.

CHAPTER 31

The Field Hospital

When he came to, it was daylight, and two stretcher bearers were tugging at his feet. The weight of him seemed terrific, but eventually they hoisted him on to the stretcher.

Some of his men gathered round, and told him that "they'd soon put him straight at the hospital."

He smiled, rather wryly, but still he smiled, and mumbled: "Well, good luck, No. 5 Platoon."

And so they carried him away, feet foremost.

They plunged along the muddy paths. He was convulsed with fear that they would overturn him. And the jolting sent red-hot pains through his head, and twisted his back terribly.

A company came straggling up the path, led by no other than the major, who had been his company commander at the beginning of the war.

"Well, young feller, how are you? You'll be all right in a day or two."

Reply was impossible for him, and the major hurried on.

The men who followed seemed shy of him. They looked at him covertly, and then turned their eyes quickly away, as if he were some horrible object. It annoyed him not a little.

That journey was the most painful thing that happened to him. But each sickening jolt had the compensation of landing him a yard nearer the hospital, and the hope of easing his pains buoyed him up somehow.

When they arrived at the Gunner's Cave, the stretcher bearers put him resolutely down, and intimated that it was not "up to them" to take him any further. The ambulance, they said, ought to be there to "take over" from them. But there was no sign of an ambulance, and meantime he was literally thirsting for the attentions and comforts of a hospital. His natural reserve broke completely down. He begged, and entreated, and prayed them to take him on.

After a little hesitation, they set out once more with a little excusable cursing and grumbling.

It was about seven o'clock when at last they laid him down in the hall of the hospital, and departed with unfeigned gladness.

Two hospital orderlies carried him along a passage and into the identical billiard-room that he had seen from the garden.

A doctor undid the soiled bandages with quick, strong fingers, and bent down to examine the wound with an expression of concentrated ferocity on his face. An orderly brought a bowl, and the doctor began to wash the place.

It was a painful business, but nothing to be compared to the pain produced by the "prober." They even tried to shave the hair from the affected spot. He bore it as long as he could. But it was too much. His left side shook and trembled. It was too terrible to begin to describe.

"It's no good," he said, "it's more than you can expect anyone to put up with. You'll have to stop it."

So they tied his head up once more, and he was carried upstairs into a bedroom. They lifted him on to the bed, managed at length to divest him of his jacket, turned some clothes over him, and left him.

★★★★★★

In an hour a raging fever had taken hold of him.

Only intermittently, during the next three or four days, did he so much as touch the world of realities. The only improvement was his face, which had to a great extent relaxed. Otherwise the pain and the paralysis were the same, and all the time the fever raged within him.

Somehow, when he awoke from his horrible dreams it was always dark. And the remarkable thing was that the same nightmares seemed to haunt him with persistent regularity. Always he lay down upon a hillside—nebulous black, and furry. Always too, he had been "left," and the enemy was swooping quickly down upon him. He would wake up to find himself once more inert upon the bed, would curse himself for a fool, and vow that never again would he allow his mind to drift towards that terrible thought again.

J.O. double F.R.E? What was it? A Name? Whose? When and Why? He would catch himself worrying about this many times. He would awake with a start, and realise that the solution was a perfectly easy matter. Then he would straightway fall asleep, to worry once again.

There was a big vase on a table near the bedside. He took an implacable dislike to it, and longed to shatter it into atoms. "Horrible pretentious affair," he would mutter.

When he awoke from his fever, he would always make frantic efforts to hang on to consciousness. To this end he would always call the orderly, ask the time, demand water or Bovril—anything to keep him a little longer in touch with the world.

Sometimes he would see bleared faces looking down upon him out of the dizzy greyness. He remembers being told that "the colonel" was coming to see him. He never knew whether it was his own colonel or some A.D.M.S.

The thought did indeed come to him that he was going mad. But he had not the power to worry about the discovery, and insensibility would claim him once more before he could realise the terrors of insanity.

All this time he lay on his back. It was impossible to move him, but he longed to lie comfortably on his side, as he had always been accustomed to do. He was sure he could sleep then—ordinary sound sleep, free from worry, phantomless, refreshing. How he longed for it!

One evening a doctor came to him and told him that they were going to move him away. The news was by no means a relief. He did not feel equal to the exertion of being carried about. He wanted to be allowed just to lie quietly where he was, and live or die, just as *fate* decreed. For anything more, he had no energy; and the prospect of another journey appalled him.

In the dead of night four silent orderlies heaved him on to a stretcher, carried him downstairs, and out of the *château*. His stretcher was then slid into an ambulance, and he awaited impatiently the filling of the others.

Another stretcher was slipped in by his side. It was too dark to see the man upon it, but he was apparently suffering from the last stages of thirst. He had been shot through the roof of the mouth and the throat, and could not swallow. He was dying of thirst and hunger. He begged and entreated them for water. He pleaded with them, tried to bribe them, tried to order them, tried to bully them. It was pitiable to hear a strong man brought so low. And if they gave him a drop of water in a teaspoon, he would cough and choke to such a degree that it was obvious that too frequent doses would be the end of him. He would gurgle, and moan, and pine. It was awful.

They were journeying to the clearing hospital. The road, bad at the best of times, was now pitted with shell holes, and was truly abominable. "Is a country," he said to himself, "that will not allow its wounded pneumatic tyres to ride upon, worth fighting for?"

They jolted on through the remaining part of the night. At dawn they were disembarked, and put to rest in a little farm-house, where they gave them soup and milk. But there were only mattresses thrown on a stone floor, and the pain in his spine was so acute that he almost forgot about his head.

His companion on the journey was placed in the same room. At the beginning of the night he had pitied the poor fellow immensely. But his prayers and entreaties were too pitiful to bear. What he must have been suffering! It added an extra weight to his own burden. Thank God, he had never been very thirsty!

"Just a little water! Just a drop. I won't swallow it. I won't! I swear before Heaven I won't! Just a teaspoonful! Please! . . . Oh! I'm dying of thirst. . . . Only a drop. . . . I won't swallow it this time. . . . There's five pounds in my pocket." He would gurgle and groan pitifully for a moment. Then in a voice, astoundingly loud, but thick with blood, he would shout, quaveringly: "Orderly, blast you, you ——, give me some water, or I'll—"

Sad to say, there came a time when the subaltern could bear it no longer. His own troubles and the entreaties of the other unnerved him.

"Give him water! Chuck it at him! In a bucket!" he shouted in a frenzy. "Let the poor wretch die happy, anyway."

The corporal in charge came over to him.

"You might get me some milk, corporal," he said.

"For you, sir?"

"Oh no! You ——, to water the plants with, of course!"

"I was only asking, sir."

"All right, corp'ral. Can't you see I'm a little upset this morning?"

★★★★★★

They carried him on to the clearing hospital in a motor ambulance, and deposited him in the hall of a little *estaminet* that had been turned into an officer's hospital.

A doctor and sister were conversing in low tones outside a closed door.

"I'm afraid there are all the symptoms of enteric," she was saying.

Neither of them took the slightest notice of him. But he was getting used to being carried about and never spoken to, like a piece of furniture. And the sister entranced him. The clearing hospitals were the nearest places to the fighting-line that women could aspire to. He had not seen an English lady since leaving England. And her waist pleased him. Such few French peasant women had any waists at all. And her voice was higher-pitched; more intellectual, if less poetic.

When the two of them had quite finished discussing their "case" she called for an orderly, and without so much as looking at him, said, "Put that one in there," indicating another door. Another orderly was fetched, and the painful business of hauling him off the stretcher on to a bed began once more.

The novelty of his surroundings occupied his mind. The bed was soft, and his spine ceased to ache. A feeling almost akin to contentment stole over him, as they left him in the clean, cool bed. His companion without the throat had been put in another room. There was only one more bed in this one, and the occupant was sleeping peacefully.

About four o'clock in the afternoon he heard the faint ring of spurred boots in the hall.

"This is an officer's ward, sir," a voice was saying.

The field-marshal commanding-in-chief, followed by another officer only less distinguished than himself, came slowly in.

"Poor boys!" he said. "How are you getting on?"

"All right, thank you, sir," he answered, smiling with pride.

"Here's the latest news from England," added the great man, as he dropped a paper on the bed. The subaltern's left hand almost shot out of bed to grasp it. He looked up just in time to see them disappearing through the doorway.

He tried to read the paper, but the effort brought the very worst pains back again to his head, so he concealed it under the coverlet of the bed. He was determined to keep that paper. It was already growing dark, when the young doctor of the ward came to his bedside, smiling.

"We are going to operate on you at eight o'clock," he said. "It will be all right. We'll soon put you straight."

"Straight?" he echoed. "Yes, I dare say you will!"

CHAPTER 32

Operation

The news came as a distinct shock to him. He had not even entertained the possibility of undergoing an operation. Years ago he had had his adenoids removed, and the memory was by no means pleasant. All along he had told himself he would recover in time—that was all he wanted. To have an operation was, he thought, to run another and unnecessary risk.

Later in the evening the sister came in with a large phial, and injected the contents into his arm.

"Morphine," she explained.

In a moment or so he felt that he did not care what happened. The morphine made him gloriously drunk.

"Sister," he confided. "I'm drunk. It isn't fair to go and kill a fellow when he's drunk, you know. It isn't playing the game. You ought to suspend hostilities till I'm sober!"

He felt ridiculously proud of himself for these inanities.

"I know you," he strutted with laughter. "After it's all over, you'll write home to my people and say, 'The operation was successfully performed, but the patient died soon afterwards!'"

By this time they had stripped him of all but his shirt.

"Where's my bier? Where's my bier? Is a gentleman to be kept waiting all night for his bier?" he exclaimed, with mock impatience.

They lifted him on to a stretcher, and began to push it through the open window into the street.

"Farewell, Ophelia!" he cried to the sister, as his head disappeared.

He was too drunk to feel afraid.

They carried him into the room that had been turned into a theatre. He found that the same young doctor was to operate on him. He was alarmed at his youth.

"I like a fellow to have white hair if he's to operate on me," he said to himself.

Another doctor began to adjust the ether apparatus.

"Look here," he mumbled, "how do you know my heart's strong enough for this sort of thing?"

"Don't be a fool; it's your only chance."

"Oh, all right. Have it your own way, only don't say I did not warn you!" he replied.

"Rather a character," said one of the doctors, as he placed the sodden wool firmly over his nose and mouth.

"Yes," replied the sister; "he said just now that the operation would be unsuccessful and that he would die!"

Drat the woman, she had spoiled his last joke!

He strove to explain. But the fumes were clutching at his senses, and he could not. The white walls of the room swam and bounced before his eyes. Rivers were pouring into his ears. Everything was grey and vibrating. He made a frantic effort to turn his thoughts towards God and home, "in case." But he failed to think of anything.

With a jerk his senses left him.

★★★★★★

When he recovered his senses it was still dark, but he realised that he was in another room.

And in that room he stayed for nearly a fortnight before the doctor would allow him to proceed to the base.

As regards the paralysis, there was little or no improvement, although he thought at one time that he was succeeding in wagging his big toe. The doctor would come in and say with mock petulance, "Surely you can move that finger now. Pull yourself together! Make an effort!"

He used to make tremendous efforts. Even his left hand used to twitch with the effort of trying to move the right.

"No, not your left; the right," the doctor would say.

Then he would laugh, and go away saying that it would be all right in time.

His chief difficulty, not counting, of course, the perpetual headache, was his inability to sleep. The nights seemed interminable, and he dreaded them. The days were only less so because of the excitement of meals and being talked to by the sister. They became fast friends, and she would tell him all about her work, her troubles with the doctors and with refractory orderlies. They used to laugh together over the short temper of a patient below, whom she used to call "Old Fiddlesticks," and who seemed to be the most impatient of patients. Then she would wander on about her home, how she nursed half the year, and spent the remainder with her married sister in Fondborough Manor.

One day one of the orderlies shaved him, and everyone was surprised "to see how much better he looked!"

They used to give him aspirin, and though it generally failed to bring sleep, his pains would be relieved almost instantly, and his spirits would rise to tremendous heights. The only time he was able to sleep seemed to be between six and ten. He was nearly always awakened by the lusty voice of a peasant entering the room beneath. He complained to the orderly, with the result that the next night the lusty voice was suddenly silenced.

"Shut yer mouth, or I'll knock yer blinking face in!" And Lusty Voice understood.

★★★★★★

At last the doctor gave his consent for removal to the base hospital, and the subaltern found himself being once more hauled on to a stretcher and heaved into the ambulance.

They dragged him out at the station, and he saw the long train, each carriage brilliantly lit. The sight seemed so civilised that it cheered him not a little.

The carriage was an ordinary "wagon-lit" converted with considerable ingenuity into a hospital train. He shared his compartment with a young *guardee*, "a sitting case."

He had no sooner settled down than a voice was heard calling for "Second-Lieutenant Hackett."

"Here," replied the *guardee*, without any enthusiasm.

A dapper staff officer, so tall that he had to stoop to enter the compartment, drew a paper from his pocket.

"You?" he asked. "Well, Hackett, this is a great evening in your life, and I congratulate you." He shook the *guardee's* left hand. "You have been given the D.S.O.," he added hurriedly, for the train had already begun to move. With that he disappeared.

It was not until the following morning that the sister came in to dress his wound.

"What strong teeth you've got, boy!" she said.

Nobody knew better than he did that his teeth were large and tended to protrude, but it is always annoying to have one's defects

139

admired.

The orderly was, in his way, an artist. He was light-handed, quick, deferential, and soothing—a prince among orderlies. He produced wonderful tit-bits—amongst other things tinned chicken, sardines, chocolate, and, for the *guardee*, stout! Three minutes after the sister had strictly forbidden him to read, the orderly smuggled into his hand the Paris *Daily Mail* of the day before. Von Moltke had been dismissed. "The first of the great failures," he said to himself. But the sister was right; it was too painful to read.

"What are we stopping here for?" the *guardee* asked once.

"To unload the dead, sir," replied the orderly, with serious suavity.

The journey took over two days. They touched at Versailles and Le Mans, the advanced base, swept slowly down the broad valley of the Loire, past the busy town of Nantes, followed by the side of the estuary, oddly mixed up with the shipping, and eventually came to rest in the town of St. Nazaire, at that time the base of the British Army.

CHAPTER 33

St. Nazaire

His next home was a comfortable little bed in a white-painted cubicle of a boys' school that had been turned into a base hospital. When at length he found himself at rest in his new bed, he sighed with contentment. Everything was so quiet, and clean, and orderly. After the dirty estaminet, and the feverish hurry of the clearing hospital, this was indeed *peace*. They gave him real broth to drink and real chicken to eat. And that night, as he sank almost for the first time into real sleep, he felt that heaven had been achieved.

Life began to creep slowly into his paralysed limbs. With infinite labour he could force his first finger and thumb to meet and separate again. His toes wagged freely. The only fly in the ointment was that the "stuff they did their dressings with" was of a fiercer nature and hurt more than the previous ones. Also, the dressings became more frequent.

He made great friends with the doctor and the sisters. One of them used to talk of an old major in his regiment with a tenderness that led him to suspect a veiled romance. He was now growing better daily, and was assailed with the insatiable hunger that follows fever. No sooner had he bolted down one meal than he counted the hours to the next.

One day they left a meal-tray on his chest, and apparently forgot it. At the end of half-an-hour his patience abandoned him. He deliberately reached out and threw everything upon the floor. The sister came running up to see what was the matter. He maintained a haughty silence. She picked up the aluminium plates and cups. Her starched dress crinkled.

"Oh, you naughty boy!" she said, smiling entrancingly.

There was nothing for it: he burst out laughing.

Soon afterwards it occurred to him that, as all he had got to do was to lie in bed and wait, this could be done just as easily in a London hospital.

"As soon as you are well enough to travel, you shall go to England. Your case can be better treated there," the doctor promised him.

CHAPTER 34

Somewhere in Mayfair

The speed of the train astounded him. Such tremendous things had happened to him since he had last travelled in an express train. He loved every English field as it passed, every hedge and tree.

He was at peace with the world. The only blemish was that the awful war was still dragging on its awful course—still exacting its awful toll. He was rushing Londonwards—towards his "people" and everything he wanted. The pains had gone from his head, except for occasional headaches. And, wonder of wonders, he could move his whole leg and arm! Contentment stole over him. He was on perfectly good terms with himself and the world in general. Life, after all, was delightful.

******

The voyage had been wonderful. Not for one moment of the forty-eight hours that it took to reach Southampton did the wavelets upset the equilibrium of the vessel. Only the faintest vibration showed him that she was moving at all. The food had been good and plentiful, the attendance matchless. All things seemed to be "working together for good."

While engrossed in this reverie, he awoke to the fact that well-known landscapes were rolling past his window.

Tidshot! There was the familiar landmark—the tree-crested hill and the church. The station flashed by, and then the well-known training areas.

"Just as if I were going up to town for the week-end!" he told himself.

The familiar suburbs whizzed past. Clapham Junction, Vauxhall, the grinding of brakes, and the train was gliding quietly along Waterloo platform.

An officer boarded the train, and, in spite of a great deal of discussion and requests, succeeded in thrusting scraps of paper into everyone's hand.

"The Something Hospital, Chester Square," someone read.

"What? Oh, I thought you said 'The Empire Hospital, Leicester Square!'" yelled half-a-dozen wits almost simultaneously.

He was carried out on his stretcher, slid into a St. John Ambulance, and driven to the address on the piece of paper, which was "not a hundred miles from Berkeley Square," as the gossip writers put it.

The ambulance stretcher bearers carried him into the hall of what was evidently a private house "turned" into a hospital. A great many ladies were standing about, all in Red Cross uniform. A man was there, too. Curiously enough, he was wearing just the coat and hat that his father would wear. Could it be possible? He turned round; lo and behold, it *was* his father!

"Hallo, Father!" he said.

The man came up.

Both of them seemed at a loss for words. It was neither emotion nor sentimentality; it was just the lack of something to say. Taking advantage of the pause, the crowd bore down upon him, and by reason of their superior numbers drove him away, offering promises about "the day after tomorrow."

They carried the subaltern upstairs, and placed him in a room where two other officers who had arrived on the same boat were already established.

The hospital was "run" by the Hon. Mrs. Blank, who was placing her entire house at the disposal of the War Office. She did everything herself: the feeding, equipping, providing the staff. The expense must have been huge. She worked night and day as general manageress of the establishment. There ought to be some special honour and knighthood for such women on this earth, and a special heaven in the next. The subaltern used to feel positively ashamed of himself when he thought of the money, kindness and care that she was lavishing upon them.

The whole hospital was a glorious, pulsating, human organisation. What was wanted was done, not what was "laid down" in some schedule. Indeed, their wishes were gratified before they had time to form in the mind. It was a fairyland, and of course the fairies were the nurses. The subaltern and his two companions held a conference on their respective merits.

"I like the little pale brown one; she's like a mouse."

"There's no comparison. Ours is the star turn."

"Which *is* ours?"

"The one who dashes about?"

"The one who upset the dinner-trays?"

"Yes. Wasn't it funny? I thought I should have died!"

The doctors, this time civilians, used to come to him twice a day. They were quiet, reserved men, positively glowing with efficiency.

They dressed his wound, tested the reflex actions of his nerves, gazed through holes in bright mirrors at his eyes, and made him watch perpendicular pencils moving horizontally across his line of vision.

But life was racing back into his limbs. Hourly his strength was returning. He no longer lay staring listlessly in the bottom of the bed. He liked now to work himself up, to lose nothing of what was going on around, to share in the talk, and, until the next headache came, to *live*.

He wallowed in the joy of reaching harbour.

Such rapid progress did he make that they began, in a few days, to treat him as a rational human being. They allowed him meat, and once, owing to a mistake on the part of the young Hurrier, a whisky-and-soda. They allowed him to smoke a restricted number of cigarettes, and to read as often as he liked. But aspirin they barred.

He had not many friends in London, so during visiting hours he was left in comparative peace.

One morning his mother came. As the door opened and she hurried into the room with her quick, bird-like grace, he felt that she was a stranger to him. Somehow their old intimacy seemed dissolved, and would have, piece by piece, to be built up again. Her round, appealing eyes of palest brown stirred him as no other eyes—even her own— had ever done before.

Her slim shoulders delighted him.

"Waddles!" he said; "you're priceless!"

He loved to call her "Waddles."

They asked the doctor when he would be likely to be able to go home.

"As soon as the wound is covered over," he replied, "there is no reason why he should not go home. Providing he could get massage and proper treatment."

★★★★★★

The gas darkly illuminated the sombre red of the walls and glimmered on the polished mahogany. The fire, too, glowed red. Outside, the wind was sighing softly in the pine-trees.

The bed seemed huge and its capacity for comfort enormous. The cool sheets seemed to caress his legs. His whole nervous system was delightfully wearied with the achievement of reaching home.

The local doctor had promised that he could treat him perfectly well, and he had been allowed to leave the hospital.

He could hear the paws of his spaniel padding softly on the carpet in the landing. He could hear the voices of his father and sister in the hall. . . .

Peace after the storm! The harbour reached at last.

"It seems to be impossible to believe it's true," he murmured to himself.

"Are you quite ready?" asked his mother.

She was standing beneath the gas-bracket, one hand raised to the handle. The light silhouetted her impertinent little nose and glimmered in her dusky hair.

Then with a jerk she turned out the light.